CAREER
IDEAS
for kids who like
WRITING

THE CAREER IDEAS FOR KIDS SERIES

Career Ideas for Kids Who Like Adventure and Travel, Second Edition
Career Ideas for Kids Who Like Animals and Nature, Second Edition
Career Ideas for Kids Who Like Art, Second Edition
Career Ideas for Kids Who Like Computers, Second Edition
Career Ideas for Kids Who Like Math and Money, Second Edition
Career Ideas for Kids Who Like Music and Dance, Second Edition
Career Ideas for Kids Who Like Science, Second Edition
Career Ideas for Kids Who Like Sports, Second Edition
Career Ideas for Kids Who Like Talking, Second Edition
Career Ideas for Kids Who Like Writing, Second Edition

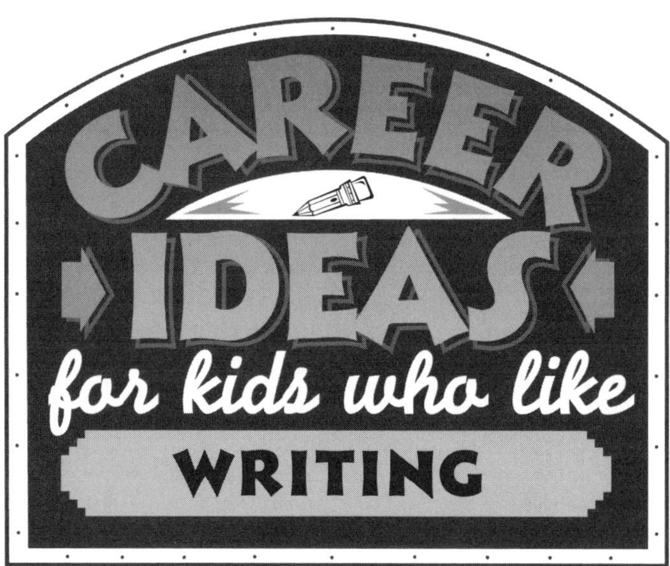

Second Edition

DIANE LINDSEY REEVES
with
LINDSEY CLASEN

Ferguson
An imprint of Infobase Publishing

CAREER IDEAS FOR KIDS WHO LIKE WRITING, Second Edition

Ferguson
An imprint of Infobase Publishing
132 West 31st Street
New York NY 10001

Library of Congress Cataloging-in-Publication Data

Reeves, Diane Lindsey, 1959-
Career ideas for kids who like writing / Diane Lindsey Reeves with Lindsey Clasen ; illustrations by Nancy Bond. — 2nd ed.
p. cm.
Includes bibliographical references and index.
ISBN-13: 978-0-8160-6555-4 (hardcover : alk. paper)
ISBN-10: 0-8160-6555-1 (hardcover : alk. paper) 1. Authorship—Vocational guidance—Juvenile literature. 2. Creative writing—Vocational guidance—Juvenile literature. 3. Book industries and trade—Vocational guidance—Juvenile literature. I. Clasen, Lindsey. II. Title.
PN151.R42 2007
808'.02023—dc22 2007003651

Ferguson books are available at special discounts when purchased in bulk quantities for businesses, associations, institutions, or sales promotions. Please call our Special Sales Department in New York at (212) 967-8800 or (800) 322-8755.

You can find Ferguson on the World Wide Web at http://www.fergpubco.com

Original text and cover design by Smart Graphics
Illustrations by Nancy Bond

Printed in the United States of America

MP Hermitage 10 9 8 7 6 5 4 3 2 1

This book is printed on acid-free paper.

CONTENTS

Special thanks to
Marilyn Pollard
for all she added to this book—
the feedback, the great interviews,
and most of all,
the friendship

A million thanks to the people who took the time to share their career stories and provide photos for this book:

Mary Ellen Bates
Debbie Becker
Chris Chavez
Wayne Crocker
Elizabeth Curtler
Chris Dealy
Paul and Sarah Edwards
Kimberle English
Ann Flower
Tom Giesen
David Hendin
Susan Lingo
Eileen O'Reilly
Clara Villarosa
Naomi Wax

Finally, much appreciation and admiration is due to all the behind-the-scenes people at Ferguson who have done so much to make this series all that it is. With extra thanks to James Chambers and Sarah Fogarty.

Choices.

You make them every day. What do I want for breakfast? Which shirt can I pull out of the dirty-clothes hamper to wear to school today? Should I finish my homework or play video games?

Some choices don't make much difference in the overall scheme of things. Face it; who really cares whether you wear the blue shirt or the red one?

Other choices are a major big deal. Figuring out what you want to be when you grow up is one of those all-important choices.

But, you say, you're just a kid. How are you supposed to know what you want to do with your life?

You're right: 10, 11, 12, and even 13 are a bit young to know exactly what and where and how you're going to do whatever it is you're going to do as an adult. But it's the perfect time to start making some important discoveries about who you are, what you like to do, and what you do best. It's a great time to start exploring the options and experimenting with different ideas. In fact, there's never a better time to mess around with different career ideas without messing up your life.

When it comes to picking a career, you've basically got two choices.

CHOICE A

You can be like lots of other people and just go with the flow. Float through school doing only what you absolutely have to in order to graduate, take any job you can find, collect a paycheck, and meander your way to retirement without making much of a splash in life.

Although many people take this route and do just fine, others end up settling for second best. They miss out on a meaningful education, satisfying work, and the rewards of a focused and well-planned career. That's why this path is not an especially good idea for someone who actually wants to have a life.

CHOICE B

Other people get a little more involved in choosing a career. They figure out what they want to accomplish in their lives—whether it's making a difference, making lots of money, or simply enjoying what they do. Then they find out what it takes to reach that goal, and they set about doing it with gusto. It's kind of like these people do things on purpose instead of letting life happen by accident.

Choosing A is like going to an ice cream parlor where there are all kinds of awesome flavors and ordering a single scoop of plain vanilla. Going with Choice B is more like visiting that same ice cream parlor and ordering a super duper brownie sundae drizzled with hot fudge, smothered in whip cream, and topped with a big red cherry.

Do you see the difference?

Reading this book is a great idea for kids who want to go after life in a big way. It provides a first step toward learning about careers that match your skills, values, and dreams. It will help you make the most out of your time in school and maybe even inspire you to—as the U.S. Army so proudly says—"be all that you can be."

Ready for the challenge of Choice B? If so, read the next section for instructions on how to get started.

This book isn't just about interesting careers that other people have. It's also a book about interesting careers that you can have.

Of course, it won't do you a bit of good to just read this book. To get the whole shebang, you're going to have to jump in with both feet, roll up your sleeves, put on your thinking cap—whatever it takes—to help you do these three things:

- Discover what you do best and enjoy the most. (This is the secret ingredient for finding work that's perfect for you.)

- Explore ways to match your interests and abilities with career ideas.
- Experiment with lots of different ideas until you find the ideal career. (It's like trying on all kinds of hats to see which ones fit!)

Use this book as a road map to some exciting career destinations. Here's what to expect in the chapters that follow.

GET IN GEAR!

First stop: discover. These activities will help you uncover important clues about the special traits and abilities that make you *you*. When you are finished you will have developed a personal Skill Set that will help guide you to career ideas in the next chapter.

TAKE A TRIP!

Next stop: explore. Cruise down the career idea highway and find out about a variety of career ideas that are especially appropriate for people who like writing. Use the Skill Set chart at the beginning of each career profile to match your own interests with those required for success on the job.

Once you've identified a career that interests you, kick your exploration into high gear by checking out some of the Web sites, library resources, and professional organizations listed at the end of each career profile. For an extra challenge, follow the instructions for the Try It Out activities.

MAKE A WRITING DETOUR!

Here's your chance to explore up-and-coming opportunities such as book packager and information broker as well as the tried-and-true routes of editor, librarian, and journalist.

Just when you thought you'd seen it all, here come dozens of interesting writing ideas to add to the career mix. Charge up your career search by learning all you can about some of these opportunities.

DON'T STOP NOW!

Third stop: experiment. The library, the telephone, a computer, and a mentor—four keys to a successful career planning adventure. Use them well, and before long you'll be on the trail of some hot career ideas of your own.

WHAT'S NEXT?

Make a plan! Chart your course (or at least the next stop) with these career planning road maps. Whether you're moving full steam ahead with a great idea or get slowed down at a yellow light of indecision, these road maps will keep you moving forward toward a great future.

Use a pencil—you're bound to make a detour or two along the way. But, hey, you've got to start somewhere.

HOORAY! YOU DID IT!

Some final rules of the road before sending you off to new adventures.

SOME FUTURE DESTINATIONS

This section lists a few career planning tools you'll want to know about.

You've got a lot of ground to cover in this phase of your career planning journey. Start your engines and get ready for an exciting adventure!

Career planning is a lifelong journey. There's usually more than one way to get where you're going, and there are often some interesting detours along the way. But you have to start somewhere. So rev up and find out all you can about one-of-a-kind, specially designed you. That's the first stop on what can be the most exciting trip of your life!

To get started, complete the five exercises described throughout the following pages.

DISCOVER #1: WATCH FOR SIGNS ALONG THE WAY

Road signs help drivers figure out how to get where they want to go. They provide clues about direction, road conditions, and safety. Your career road signs will provide clues about who you are, what you like, and what you do best. These clues can help you decide where to look for the career ideas that are best for you.

Complete the following statements to make them true for you. There are no right or wrong reasons. Jot down the response that describes you best. Your answers will provide important clues about career paths you should explore.

Please Note: If this book does not belong to you, write your responses on a separate sheet of paper.

On my last report card, I got the best grade in ______________ .

On my last report card, I got the worst grade in ______________ .

I am happiest when ______________________ .

Something I can do for hours without getting bored is ______________________ .

Something that bores me out of my mind is ______________________________ .

My favorite class is ____________________ .

My least favorite class is ________________ .

The one thing I'd like to accomplish with my life is ____________________________ .

My favorite thing to do after school is ______________________________________ .

My least favorite thing to do after school is ____________________________ .

Something I'm really good at is _______ .

Something really tough for me to do is ______________________________ .

My favorite adult person is ______________ because ______________________________ .

When I grow up ________________________ .

The kinds of books I like to read are about ______________________________ .

The kinds of videos I like to watch are about ________________________________ .

DISCOVER #2: RULES OF THE ROAD

Pretty much any job you can think of involves six common ingredients. Whether the work requires saving the world or selling bananas, all work revolves around a central **purpose** or reason for existing. All work is conducted somewhere, in some **place**, whether it's on the 28th floor of a city skyscraper or on a cruise ship in the middle of an ocean. All work requires a certain **time** commitment and is performed using various types of **tools**. **People** also play an important part in most jobs—whether the job involves interacting with lots or very few of them. And, especially from where you are sitting as a kid still in school, all work involves some type of **preparation** to learn how to do the job.

Another word for these six common ingredients is *values.* Each one represents important aspects of work that people value in different ways. The following activity will give you a chance to think about what matters most to you in each of these areas. That way you'll get a better idea of things to look for as you explore different careers.

Here's how the process works:

First, read the statements listed for each value on the following pages. Decide which, if any, represent your idea of an ideal job.

Next, take a look at the grid on page 15. For every value statement with which you agreed, draw its symbol in the appropriate space on your grid. (If this book doesn't belong to you, use a blank sheet of paper to draw your own grid with six big spaces.) Or, if you want to get really fancy, cut pictures out of magazines and glue them into the appropriate space. If you do not see a symbol that represents your best answer, make up a new one and sketch it in the appropriate box.

When you are finished, you'll have a very useful picture of the kinds of values that matter most to you in your future job.

PURPOSE Which of the following statements describes what you most hope to accomplish in your future work? Pick as many as are true for you and feel free to add others.		
	❑	I want to help other people.
	❑	I want to make lots of money.
	❑	I want to do something I really believe in.
	❑	I want to make things.
	❑	I want to use my brain power in challenging ways.
	❑	I want to work with my own creative ideas.
	❑	I want to be very successful.
	❑	I want to find a good company and stick with it for the rest of my life.
	❑	I want to be famous.
Other purpose-related things that are especially important to me are		

PLACE When you think about your future work, what kind of place would you most like to do it in? Pick as many as are true for you and feel free to add others.		
	❑	I want to work in a big city skyscraper.
	❑	I want to work in a shopping mall or retail store.
	❑	I want to work in the great outdoors.
	❑	I want to travel a lot for my work.
	❑	I want to work out of my own home.
	❑	I want to work for a government agency.
	❑	I want to work in a school or university.
	❑	I want to work in a factory or laboratory.
Other place-related things that are especially important to me are		

TIME

When you think about your future work, what kind of schedule sounds most appealing to you? Pick as many as are true for you and feel free to add others.

	❑	I'd rather work regular business hours—nine to five, Monday through Friday.
	❑	I'd like to have lots of vacation time.
	❑	I'd prefer a flexible schedule so I can balance my work, family, and personal needs.
	❑	I'd like to work nights only so my days are free.
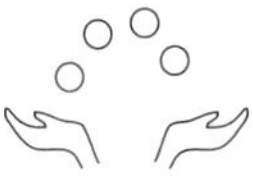	❑	I'd like to work where the pace is fast and I stay busy all day.
	❑	I'd like to work where I would always know exactly what I'm supposed to do.
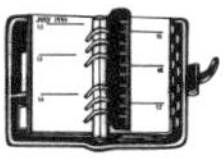	❑	I'd like to work where I could plan my own day.
	❑	I'd like to work where there's lots of variety and no two days are alike.
Other time-related things that are especially important to me are		

TOOLS What kinds of things would you most like to work with? Pick as many as are true for you and feel free to add others.		
	❑	I'd prefer to work mostly with people.
	❑	I'd prefer to work mostly with technology.
	❑	I'd prefer to work mostly with machines.
	❑	I'd prefer to work mostly with products people buy.
	❑	I'd prefer to work mostly with planes, trains, automobiles, or other things that go.
	❑	I'd prefer to work mostly with ideas.
	❑	I'd prefer to work mostly with information.
	❑	I'd prefer to work mostly with nature.
Other tool-related things that are especially important to me are		

PEOPLE

What role do other people play in your future work? How many do you want to interact with on a daily basis? What age group would you most enjoy working with? Pick as many as are true for you and feel free to add others.

	❑	I'd like to work with lots of people all day long.
	❑	I'd prefer to work alone most of the time.
	❑	I'd like to work as part of a team.
	❑	I'd like to work with people I might choose as friends.
	❑	I'd like to work with babies, children, or teenagers.
	❑	I'd like to work mostly with elderly people.
	❑	I'd like to work mostly with people who are in trouble.
	❑	I'd like to work mostly with people who are ill.

Other people-related things that are especially important to me are

PREPARATION When you think about your future work, how much time and energy do you want to devote to preparing for it? Pick as many as are true for you and feel free to add others.		
	❑	I want to find a job that requires a college degree.
	❑	I want to find a job where I could learn what I need to know on the job.
	❑	I want to find a job that requires no additional training after I graduate from high school.
	❑	I want to find a job where the more education I get, the better my chances for a better job.
BOSS	❑	I want to run my own business and be my own boss.
Other preparation-related things that are especially important to me are		

Now that you've uncovered some word clues about the types of values that are most important to you, use the grid on the following page (or use a separate sheet of paper if this book does not belong to you) to "paint a picture" of your ideal future career. Use the icons as ideas for how to visualize each statement. Or, if you'd like to get really creative, get a large sheet of paper, some markers, magazines, and glue or tape and create a collage.

PURPOSE	PLACE	TIME
TOOLS	**PEOPLE**	**PREPARATION**

DISCOVER #3: DANGEROUS DETOURS

Half of figuring out what you do want to do is figuring out what you don't want to do. Get a jump start on this process by making a list of 10 careers you already know you absolutely don't want to do.

Warning: Failure to heed early warnings signs to avoid careers like this can result in long hours of boredom and frustration spent doing a job you just weren't meant to do.

(If this book does not belong to you, make your list on a separate sheet of paper.)

1. ______________________ ______________________
2. ______________________ ______________________
3. ______________________ ______________________

4. ______________________ ______________________

5. ______________________ ______________________

6. ______________________ ______________________

7. ______________________ ______________________

8. ______________________ ______________________

9. ______________________ ______________________

10. ______________________ ______________________

Red Flag Summary:
Look over your list, and in the second column above (or on a separate sheet of paper) see if you can summarize what it is about these jobs that makes you want to avoid them like a bad case of cooties.

DISCOVER #4: ULTIMATE CAREER DESTINATION

Imagine that your dream job is like a favorite tourist destination, and you have to convince other people to pick it over every other career in the world. How would you describe it? What features make it especially appealing to you? What does a person have to do to have a career like it?

Take a blank sheet of paper and fold it into thirds. Fill each column on both sides with words and pictures that create a vivid image of what you'd most like your future career to be.

Special note: Just for now, instead of actually naming a specific career, describe what your ideal career would be like. In places where the name of the career would be used, leave a blank space like this ______________. For instance: For people who want to become rich and famous, being a ______________ is the way to go.

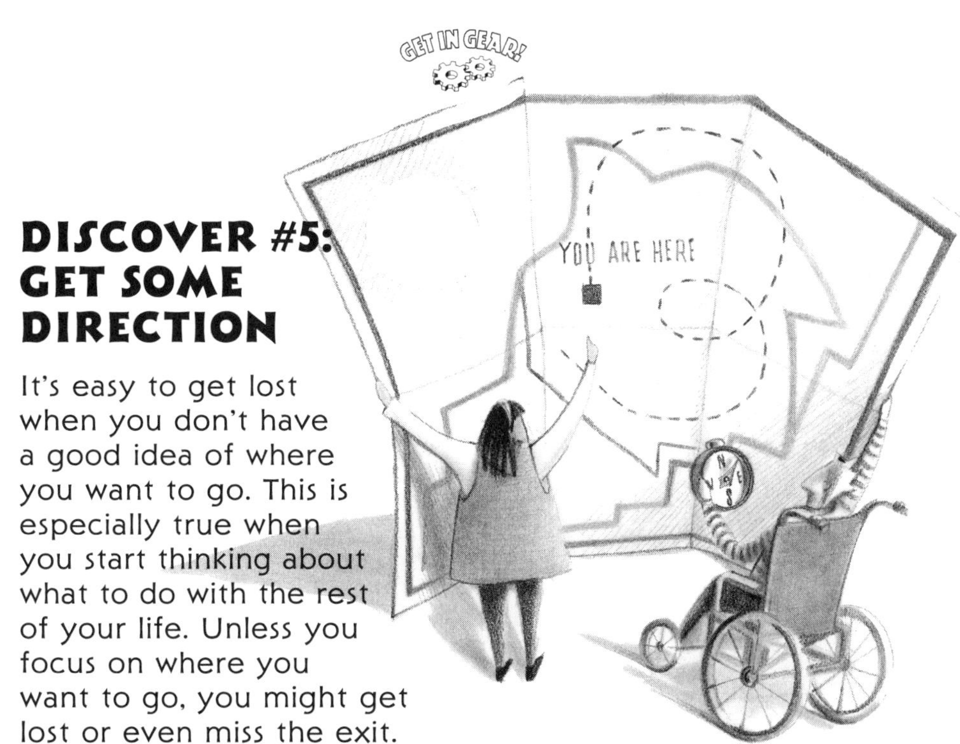

DISCOVER #5: GET SOME DIRECTION

It's easy to get lost when you don't have a good idea of where you want to go. This is especially true when you start thinking about what to do with the rest of your life. Unless you focus on where you want to go, you might get lost or even miss the exit. This discover exercise will help you connect your own interests and abilities with a whole world of career opportunities.

Mark the activities that you enjoy doing or would enjoy doing if you had the chance. Be picky. Don't mark ideas that you wish you would do. Mark only those that you would really do. For instance, if skydiving sounds appealing but you'd never do it because you are terrified of heights, don't mark it.

Please Note: If this book does not belong to you, write your responses on a separate sheet of paper.

❑ 1. Rescue a cat stuck in a tree
❑ 2. Visit the pet store every time you go to the mall
❑ 3. Paint a mural on the cafeteria wall
❑ 4. Run for student council
❑ 5. Send e-mail to a "pen pal" in another state
❑ 6. Survey your classmates to find out what they do after school
❑ 7. Try out for the school play
❑ 8. Dissect a frog and identify the different organs
❑ 9. Play baseball, soccer, football, or ________ (fill in your favorite sport)

- ❑ 10. Talk on the phone to just about anyone who will talk back
- ❑ 11. Try foods from all over the world—Thailand, Poland, Japan, etc.
- ❑ 12. Write poems about things that are happening in your life
- ❑ 13. Create a really scary haunted house to take your friends through on Halloween
- ❑ 14. Recycle all your family's trash
- ❑ 15. Bake a cake and decorate it for your best friend's birthday
- ❑ 16. Sell enough advertisements for the school yearbook to win a trip to Walt Disney World
- ❑ 17. Simulate an imaginary flight through space on your computer screen
- ❑ 18. Build model airplanes, boats, doll houses, or anything from kits
- ❑ 19. Teach your friends a new dance routine
- ❑ 20. Watch the stars come out at night and see how many constellations you can find
- ❑ 21. Watch baseball, soccer, football, or _____ (fill in your favorite sport) on TV
- ❑ 22. Give a speech in front of the entire school
- ❑ 23. Plan the class field trip to Washington, D.C.
- ❑ 24. Read everything in sight, including the back of the cereal box
- ❑ 25. Figure out "who dunnit" in a mystery story
- ❑ 26. Take in stray or hurt animals
- ❑ 27. Make a poster announcing the school football game
- ❑ 28. Think up a new way to make the lunch line move faster and explain it to the cafeteria staff
- ❑ 29. Put together a multimedia show for a school assembly using music and lots of pictures and graphics
- ❑ 30. Invest your allowance in the stock market and keep track of how it does
- ❑ 31. Go to the ballet or opera every time you get the chance
- ❑ 32. Do experiments with a chemistry set
- ❑ 33. Keep score at your sister's Little League game

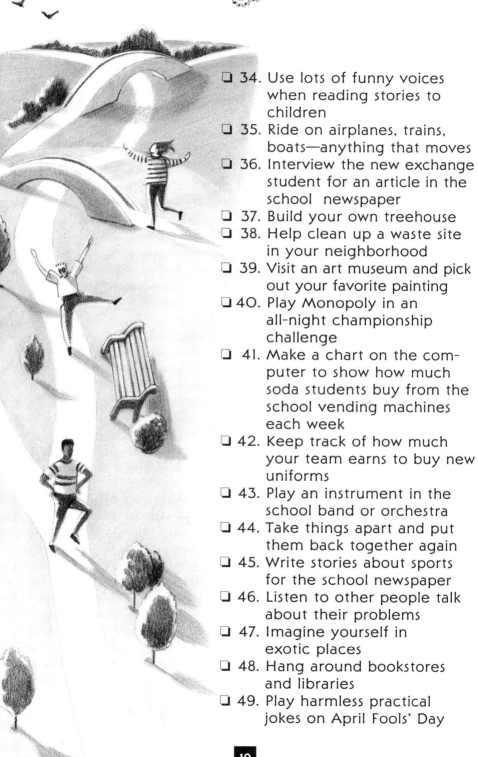

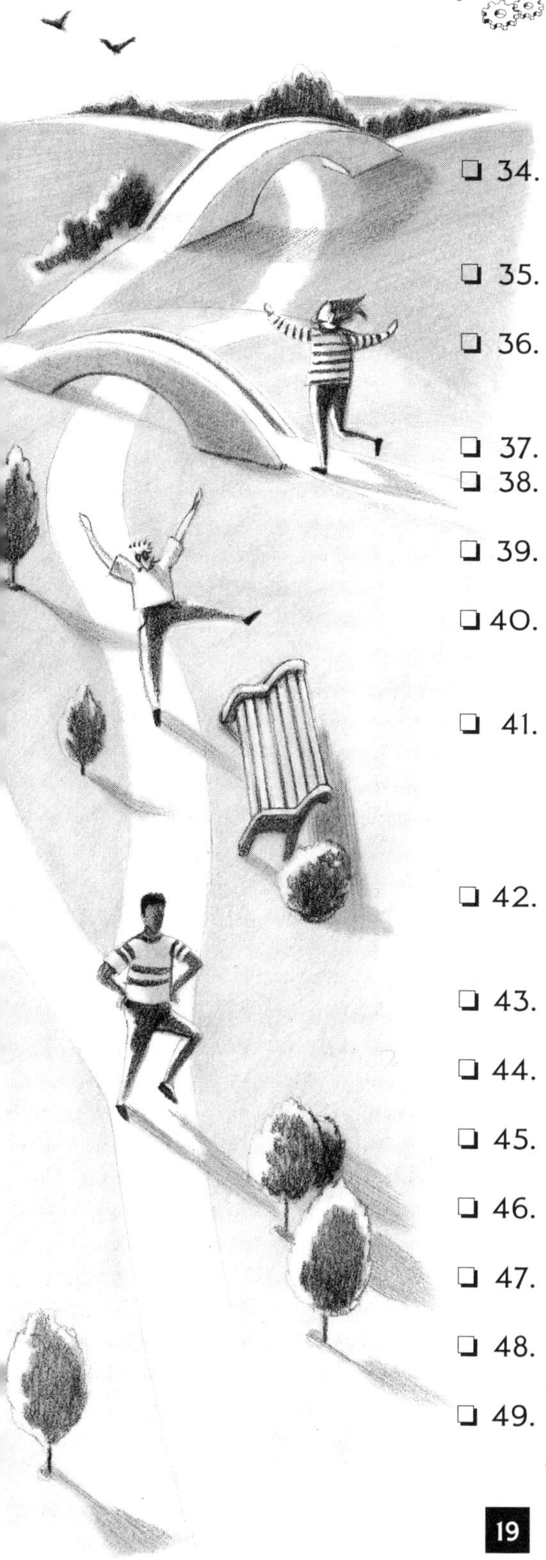

- ❏ 34. Use lots of funny voices when reading stories to children
- ❏ 35. Ride on airplanes, trains, boats—anything that moves
- ❏ 36. Interview the new exchange student for an article in the school newspaper
- ❏ 37. Build your own treehouse
- ❏ 38. Help clean up a waste site in your neighborhood
- ❏ 39. Visit an art museum and pick out your favorite painting
- ❏ 40. Play Monopoly in an all-night championship challenge
- ❏ 41. Make a chart on the computer to show how much soda students buy from the school vending machines each week
- ❏ 42. Keep track of how much your team earns to buy new uniforms
- ❏ 43. Play an instrument in the school band or orchestra
- ❏ 44. Take things apart and put them back together again
- ❏ 45. Write stories about sports for the school newspaper
- ❏ 46. Listen to other people talk about their problems
- ❏ 47. Imagine yourself in exotic places
- ❏ 48. Hang around bookstores and libraries
- ❏ 49. Play harmless practical jokes on April Fools' Day

- ❑ 50. Join the 4-H club at your school
- ❑ 51. Take photographs at the school talent show
- ❑ 52. Make money by setting up your own business—paper route, lemonade stand, etc.
- ❑ 53. Create an imaginary city using a computer
- ❑ 54. Do 3-D puzzles
- ❑ 55. Keep track of the top 10 songs of the week
- ❑ 56. Read about famous inventors and their inventions
- ❑ 57. Make play-by-play announcements at the school football game
- ❑ 58. Answer the phones during a telethon to raise money for orphans
- ❑ 59. Be an exchange student in another country
- ❑ 60. Write down all your secret thoughts and favorite sayings in a journal
- ❑ 61. Jump out of an airplane (with a parachute, of course)
- ❑ 62. Plant and grow a garden in your backyard (or windowsill)
- ❑ 63. Use a video camera to make your own movies

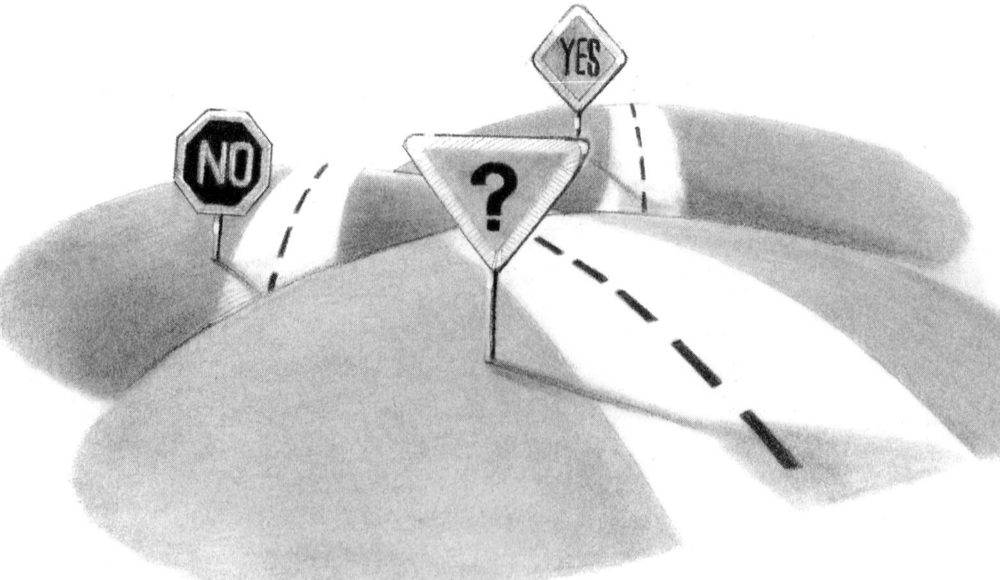

- ❏ 64. Get your friends together to help clean up your town after a hurricane
- ❏ 65. Spend your summer at a computer camp learning lots of new computer programs
- ❏ 66. Build bridges, skyscrapers, and other structures out of LEGOs
- ❏ 67. Plan a concert in the park for little kids
- ❏ 68. Collect different kinds of rocks
- ❏ 69. Help plan a sports tournament
- ❏ 70. Be DJ for the school dance
- ❏ 71. Learn how to fly a plane or sail a boat
- ❏ 72. Write funny captions for pictures in the school yearbook
- ❏ 73. Scuba dive to search for buried treasure
- ❏ 74. Recognize and name several different breeds of cats, dogs, and other animals
- ❏ 75. Sketch pictures of your friends

- ❑ 76. Pick out neat stuff to sell at the school store
- ❑ 77. Answer your classmates' questions about how to use the computer
- ❑ 78. Draw a map showing how to get to your house from school
- ❑ 79. Make up new words to your favorite songs
- ❑ 80. Take a hike and name the different kinds of trees, birds, or flowers
- ❑ 81. Referee intramural basketball games
- ❑ 82. Join the school debate team
- ❑ 83. Make a poster with postcards from all the places you went on your summer vacation
- ❑ 84. Write down stories that your grandparents tell you about when they were young

DISCOVER #6: CALCULATE THE CLUES

Now is your chance to add it all up. Each of the 12 boxes on the following pages contains an interest area that is common to both your world and the world of work. Follow these directions to discover your personal Skill Set:

1. Find all of the numbers that you checked on pages 18–23 in the following boxes and mark

them with an X. Work your way all the way through number 84.

2. Go back and count the Xs marked for each interest area. Write that number in the space that says "Total."
3. Find the interest area with the highest total and put a number one in the "Rank" blank of that box. Repeat this process for the next two highest scoring areas. Rank the second highest as number two and the third highest as number three.
4. If you have more than three strong areas, choose the three that are most important and interesting to you.

Remember: If this book does not belong to you, write your responses on a separate sheet of paper.

ADVENTURE

- ❑ 1
- ❑ 13
- ❑ 25
- ❑ 37
- ❑ 49
- ❑ 61
- ❑ 73

Total: _____
Rank: _____

ANIMALS & NATURE

- ❑ 2
- ❑ 14
- ❑ 26
- ❑ 38
- ❑ 50
- ❑ 62
- ❑ 74

Total: _____
Rank: _____

ART

- ❑ 3
- ❑ 15
- ❑ 27
- ❑ 39
- ❑ 51
- ❑ 63
- ❑ 75

Total: _____
Rank: _____

BUSINESS

- ❑ 4
- ❑ 16
- ❑ 28
- ❑ 40
- ❑ 52
- ❑ 64
- ❑ 76

Total: _____

Rank: _____

COMPUTERS

- ❑ 5
- ❑ 17
- ❑ 29
- ❑ 41
- ❑ 53
- ❑ 65
- ❑ 77

Total: _____

Rank: _____

MATH

- ❑ 6
- ❑ 18
- ❑ 30
- ❑ 42
- ❑ 54
- ❑ 66
- ❑ 78

Total: _____

Rank: _____

MUSIC/DANCE

- ❑ 7
- ❑ 19
- ❑ 31
- ❑ 43
- ❑ 55
- ❑ 67
- ❑ 79

Total: _____

Rank: _____

SCIENCE

- ❑ 8
- ❑ 20
- ❑ 32
- ❑ 44
- ❑ 56
- ❑ 68
- ❑ 80

Total: _____

Rank: _____

SPORTS

- ❑ 9
- ❑ 21
- ❑ 33
- ❑ 45
- ❑ 57
- ❑ 69
- ❑ 81

Total: _____

Rank: _____

TALKING

- ❑ 10
- ❑ 22
- ❑ 34
- ❑ 46
- ❑ 58
- ❑ 70
- ❑ 82

Total: _____

Rank: _____

TRAVEL

- ❑ 11
- ❑ 23
- ❑ 35
- ❑ 47
- ❑ 59
- ❑ 71
- ❑ 83

Total: _____

Rank: _____

WRITING

- ❑ 12
- ❑ 24
- ❑ 36
- ❑ 48
- ❑ 60
- ❑ 72
- ❑ 84

Total: _____

Rank: _____

What are your top three interest areas? List them here (or on a separate piece of paper).

1. ______________________________
2. ______________________________
3. ______________________________

This is your personal Skill Set and provides important clues about the kinds of work you're most likely to enjoy. Remember it and look for career ideas with a Skill Set that matches yours most closely. You'll find a Skill Set box at the beginning of each career profile in the following section.

Cruise down the career idea highway and enjoy in-depth profiles of some of the interesting options in this field. Keep in mind all that you've discovered about yourself so far. Find the careers that match your own Skill Set first. After that, keep on trucking through the other ideas—exploration is the name of this game.

Writing careers are based on exceptionally good communication skills. Keep in mind that writing and talking skills tend to go hand in hand (sort of like shoes and socks). If you're going to make your living as a communicator, make sure to work on both sides of the communication process.

Meanwhile, as you read about the following careers, imagine yourself doing each job and ask yourself the following questions:

- Would I like it?
- Would I be good at it?
- Is it the stuff my career dreams are made of?

If so, make a quick exit to explore what it involves, try it out, check it out, and get acquainted! Look out for the symbols below.

Buckle up and enjoy the trip!

A NOTE ON WEB SITES

Internet sites tend to move around the Web a bit. If you have trouble finding a particular site, use an Internet browser to find a specific Web site or type of information.

Advertising Copywriter

SKILL SET

- ✔ ART
- ✔ BUSINESS
- ✔ WRITING

SHORTCUTS

GO billboard hunting to see how copywriters make a few choice words pay off in sky-high signs.

READ advertisements in magazines and newspapers to see copywriters' work in print.

TRY writing an ad to promote the best things about your school.

WHAT IS AN ADVERTISING COPYWRITER?

Believe it or not, you make many decisions under the influence of advertising copywriters. Choices about the brand of clothes you wear, the fast food you eat, the movies you watch, and the games you play, as well as many other decisions, are sometimes the direct result of effective advertising. Copywriters write the words that accompany advertisements, commercials, newspaper and magazine articles, and other sales materials. Good copy (advertising and publishing lingo for the text) informs, educates, entertains, and sells—often in fewer than 10 words.

The copywriter is a vital part of an advertising team that links businesses and their products to consumers and their pocketbooks. Bottom line: Copywriting is salesmanship. Copywriters attempt to persuade consumers to buy a particular product or brand of product. According to the American Association of Advertising Agencies, copywriting is art and science, show business and just plain business, all rolled into one.

Effective copywriters know their words and know how to use them. Quite often the deadlines are tight, and a copywriter has to come up with a variety of clever and creative ideas quickly. In addition to having outstanding writing skills, a copywriter has to understand people and what motivates them to make purchasing decisions. They also have to understand business and effective ways to help businesses introduce products and services to the marketplace.

Advertising Copywriter

Copywriters work in advertising agencies of all sizes, including everything from a one-person operation to an international corporation that employs thousands of people. They often work for nonprofit organizations as well as television and radio stations, newspapers, and magazines. Experienced copywriters with good contacts often find success as freelancers, which means they work on their own for a variety of clients. Since virtually every business in the world requires advertisement services of one kind or another, the career prospects for talented copywriters are extremely good.

Technically speaking, a college degree isn't necessarily required to become a copywriter; however, in the real scheme of things, a college degree is recommended. Most of the better ad agencies look for a solid background (and college degree) in areas such as English, journalism, mass communication, advertising, marketing, or public relations.

Even more important than a degree is a proven ability to write good copy. Copywriters sell their skills with a portfolio full of creative writing samples. Samples can reflect paid work developed for a client or company as well as ideas developed for classes or for practice. It is even acceptable to develop samples by starting with an existing ad campaign and adding one's own twist to it, as long as the ideas are original and very good.

Copywriting can be an important first step toward other kinds of writing or the answer to a lucrative long-term career. It really depends on a copywriter's talent and goals. If creative writing in a fast-paced business environment appeals to you, take the advice of one successful copywriter and "just do it"!

TRY IT OUT

SCRUB-A-DUB-DUB

You've been hired to create an ad featuring your favorite brand of shampoo or soap. Come up with a snappy slogan and some snazzy pictures or graphics that would make kids your age want to buy this product. Put your ideas together to create a magazine advertisement.

MAKING THE GRADE

To do this activity, gather the following materials: blank sheets of paper, a stack of magazines, some scissors, tape or glue, and something to write with. To begin, thumb through the magazines and tear out 10 advertisements that catch your eye. Make three piles according to how you like them, with the best ads in one pile, the okay ads in another pile, and the really awful ads in the last one.

Tape or glue each ad to the middle of a piece of paper, leaving room around all four sides of the ads for you to make comments. On the best ads, use arrows and brief comments to point out the things you like best about the ads. On the okay ads, use arrows and brief comments to point out both the things you like about the ads and the things you don't like.

With all that practice under your belt, get ready to flex some advertising muscle with the last batch—the really awful ads. This time, you be the advertising copywriter! Cross out anything in the ad that just doesn't work—the headline, images, or text. Use arrows to indicate where to place your own great ideas for memorable headlines, knock-your-socks-off graphics, and killer text.

When you've finished with all three piles, put them all together to create the beginnings of your very first professional portfolio.

✔ CHECK IT OUT

ON THE WEB

GET THE INSIDE SCOOP

Copywriters everywhere stay current with what's going on in the industry by reading *AdWeek* (http://www.adweek.com). Go online and catch up on the latest news. While you're at it, stop by the Web sites of some of these world famous advertising agencies and see if you recognize any of their work:

- BBDO at http://www.bbdo.com
- Ogilvy & Mather at http://www.ogilvy.com
- Saatchi and Saatchi at http://www.saatchi.com/worldwide/fast_track.asp
- Wieden + Kennedy at http://www.wk.com
- Young & Rubicam at http://www.yr.com

ONLINE ADS

When it comes to advertising, the Internet is one of the hottest spots in town. Not only can you find helpful information about the profession itself, you can also find literally millions of examples of really creative advertising ideas. Here are a few ways to start your Internet hunt:

- Find out what happens when medicine meets Madison Avenue (this street in New York City is considered *the* advertising capital of the world) at http://scriptorium.lib.duke.edu/mma.
- Get media smart with tips found at the PBS Don't Buy It Web site at http://pbskids.org/dontbuyit.
- Check out over 50 years of Coca-Cola advertising history at http://memory.loc.gov/ammem/ccmphtml/colahome.html.
- See *Ad Week*'s best ad spots at http://www.adweek.com/aw/creative/best_spots/index.jsp.
- Goof off at the Wacky Packages Web site at http://www.wackypackages.com.

- Find out how some of your favorite companies promote themselves online by using an Internet search engine like http://www.google.com or http://www.yahoo.com to look for their Web sites by name (for instance, for Nike, look for *Nike*; for McDonalds, search for *McDonalds*; and so on).

AT THE LIBRARY

COPY READING

Find out more about the world of advertising in books such as:

Gifford, Clive. *Advertising and Marketing: Developing the Marketplace.* Chicago, Ill.: Heinemann, 2005.

Graydon, Shari, and Warren Clark. *Made You Look: How Advertising Works and Why You Should Know.* Toronto, Ont.: Annick, 2003.

Hogya, Bernie, and Sal Taibi. *Milk Mustache Mania: An Inside Look at One of Your Favorite Ad Campaigns.* New York: Scholastic, 2002.

Mierau, Christina. *Accept No Substitutes: The History of American Advertising.* Minneapolis, Minn.: Lerner, 2003.

Milton, Bess. *Advertising.* New York: Scholastic, 2004.

Petley, Julian. *Advertising.* Mankato, Minn.: Smart Apple, 2004.

Stevens, Chambers. *The Ultimate Commercial Book for Kids and Teens.* South Pasadena, Calif.: Sandcastle, 2005.

WITH THE EXPERTS

The Advertising Club of New York
235 Park Avenue South, 6th Floor
New York, NY 10003-1450
http://www.theadvertisingclub.org

Advertising Research Foundation
432 Park Avenue South
New York, NY 10016-8013
http://www.thearf.org

Advertising Women of New York
25 West 45th Street, Suite 403
New York, NY 10036-4910
http://www.awny.org

American Advertising Federation
1101 Vermont Avenue NW, Suite 500
Washington, DC 20005-6306
http://www.aaf.org

American Association of Advertising Agencies
405 Lexington Avenue, 18th Floor
New York, NY 10174-1801
http://www.aaaa.org

GET ACQUAINTED

Chris Dealy, Advertising Copywriter

CAREER PATH

CHILDHOOD ASPIRATION: To be an actor and a professional soccer player.

FIRST JOB: Dishwasher for Swenson's Ice Cream Parlor.

CURRENT JOB: Copywriter for advertising agency, actor in television commercials, and performer with an improvisational comedy group.

SOCCER WAS HIS FIRST LOVE

Chris Dealy grew up and graduated from high school in Washington, D.C. He was a star soccer player in high school and was looking forward to receiving a sports scholarship from a major college. Unfortunately, during his senior year, he broke his back while playing soccer, and his dream of a scholarship from a major college came to an end.

LIFE GOES ON

Dealy did, however, receive a scholarship from Denison University, a small school in Granville, Ohio, where he continued playing soccer. He spent his junior year in Italy studying and playing soccer. He graduated from Denison with majors in English and creative writing.

FROM THE BUCKEYE STATE TO THE ROCKIES

The two big questions facing any new college graduate are where to go and what to do. Since his girlfriend lived in a Colorado ski town, both questions were settled rather quickly. Dealy moved to Breckenridge, Colorado, where he became a self-described ski bum. It was fun for a while, but he eventually reached a point at which he wanted to put to use his college education.

He then moved to New York City, where he worked with a public relations firm. It didn't take long to discover that the Big Apple was just not the place for him. A move to Washington, D.C., followed. There, he taught creative writing and physical education in an elementary school.

BACK TO THE DRAWING BOARD AND INTO THE LIMELIGHT

Dealy taught for a year, but he still wasn't satisfied that he'd found the right career spot. So he returned to Denver and went to work as an intern in an advertising agency. The internship developed into a full-time job writing advertising copy. He now writes print, television, and radio commercials for major national clients. The agency where Dealy works is very community-spirited and does a lot of pro bono (that means free) work for good causes. This gives Dealy a welcome opportunity to work with cultural and arts organizations in Colorado.

Through this connection Dealy became closely involved in the theater community. Responding to his childhood desire to be an actor, Dealy enrolled in an improvisational acting class and found that he had a talent for performing. He now does five shows a week with a comedy improvisational theater troupe.

GETTING IT ALL TOGETHER

Besides his advertising and comedy work, Dealy uses his talents as an actor in radio and television commercials. He does commercials for such clients as State Farm Insurance, National Car Rental Company, Taco John's, and PBS (the Public Broadcasting System). All together, his writing, performing, and acting combine to make the most of his talents and education.

WORDS OF WISDOM FOR FUTURE COPYWRITERS

Dealy admits to taking a few detours along his career path; however, he is quick to point out that everything he did helped prepare him for what he's doing now. He took a roundabout route to reach this career destination, but he is now making a good living as a writer. And he loves his extracurricular work as a performer.

Dealy's advice for aspiring copywriters:

- Don't be too hard on yourself.
- Do what you like to do until you don't like doing it anymore.
- Get a well-rounded education and participate in school activities that involve writing—the school newspaper, yearbook, etc.
- Have a keen sense of curiosity and be creative in all you do.

It may take a few different turns to get where you want to be. Just follow your dream, no matter how many setbacks there might be.

Author

SKILL SET

- ✔ ADVENTURE
- ✔ TALKING
- ✔ WRITING

SHORTCUTS

GO to the library and pick out something totally different from anything you've ever read before.

READ *Conversations With J.K. Rowling* by J.K. Rowling and Lindsey Fraser (New York: Scholastic, 2001).

TRY keeping track of the bestselling children's books each week. See the *New York Times* list at (http://www.nytimes.com/pages/books/bestseller/index.html) and click on "children's books."

WHAT IS AN AUTHOR?

In the most literal sense, anyone who sits down and puts enough words on paper to compose a book is an author. Having readers, or an audience of people who will pay for the opportunity to read that book, is the one very significant detail that separates the wanna-bes from the professionals.

It's quite typical for people to associate being an author with writing novels of one kind or another. It's true that some fiction book authors make a sizable income writing best-selling novels. There are a number of authors who make frequent appearances on best-seller lists. A fortunate few even see their books made into Hollywood movies. These examples of success make writing appear quite glamorous and exciting; however, it can be misleading. The fact of the matter is that very few authors reach this level of success. There are about 15 slots on the *New York Times* fiction best-seller list. Multiply that by 52 weeks each year and compare the results with the 30,000 or so books that are published every year in the United States. No matter how you figure it, writing a novel is not a sure-fire way to get rich quick.

That is not to say that writing fiction cannot be a rewarding and worthwhile way to make a living as a writer. There are many successful fiction writers who make a comfortable living without all the fanfare of the best-seller lists. These authors tend to specialize in a particular genre, or category, of book, such as mystery, romance, Western, and science fiction, or in writing for a particular audience, such as children or young adults. The secret to success in this area is understanding the interests of a particular audience and writing books that audience will enjoy reading.

Writing fiction is just one way to earn a living as a writer. Nonfiction books offer an immensely broad and interesting arena for talented writers. Nonfiction books run the gamut from sports trivia and cookbooks to travel guides and school textbooks. Nonfiction writers tend to specialize in fields in which they have some expertise or interest. Business, science, education, and computers are some of the areas that a nonfiction writer might focus on.

Surprising as it may seem, nonfiction book authors can often earn significantly more income than fiction book authors. This is because the "shelf life" of a fiction book is often quite short. Fiction books generally have a very brief window of opportunity to sell—as short as a few weeks and usually not

much longer than a year. Those that don't catch on quickly are replaced by the constant flow of new titles. On the other hand, a nonfiction book with a well-defined audience and purpose can continue to sell over any number of years. As long as the book continues to sell, the author continues to earn royalties (a percentage of the price of each book sold, which is paid to the author).

Whether they specialize in fiction or nonfiction, some of the most successful authors are those who find ways to combine their writing with other income-producing activities. Quite often these activities are directly related to their writing and involve public speaking of one sort or another. Teaching college courses or workshops, speaking at conferences and business meetings, and producing audio training materials are just a few of the more common ways that authors supplement their incomes.

As is often the case, there is more than one route to becoming an author. Some people pursue college degrees in journalism or English. Others have degrees in a particular specialty such as business, science, or education, and they write books related to that particular field. Still others find that their educational background has no link whatsoever to what they write. Instead, they write from their own life experiences or observations. Regardless of the educational route an author chooses, he or she must possess three key skills: the ability to write, a steady flow of good ideas, and the self-discipline to actually sit down and write a good book.

CHARACTER SKETCH

Imagine that you are a famous author and that you are in the process of creating characters for a new series of books. Think of a character you'd enjoy reading about and use a blank sheet of paper to answer the following questions:

- What is the character's name?
- What does the character look like?

- What does the character like to do in his or her spare time?
- What are you likely to find in the character's pocket or purse?
- What kinds of problems or situations will your character deal with in the new books?

Use descriptive words to paint as vivid a picture of this character as possible.

DEAR DIARY

Keeping a diary or journal is a great way to practice your writing skills. Not only does it give you a chance to record thoughts and observations about life as you see it, but it also helps you develop the self-discipline of writing regularly. Buy yourself a nice notebook or journal. Make yourself write something in it every day.

Your daily contributions can be as varied as your days. One day you might think through a sticky personal problem on paper, and another day you might record a funny joke you heard or an interesting new word. It's your life and your journal—make the most of it.

TOP 10 LIST

The *New York Times* isn't the only place to find a bestselling book list. You can come up with your own. First, think about your favorite books to read when you were a little kid. Make a list of your favorite 10 titles. If you need help with official titles or author's names, go online to resources like Amazon (http://www.amazon.com) or Barnes and Noble (http://www.bn.com) and click on "children's books" to search for specific titles.

Next make a list of the 10 best books you've read recently.

Now see if you can come up with a list of 10 books you'd like to read but don't think anyone has written yet. Pick a title and subtitle to describe what the book is all about. With a little luck and lots of hard work, one of these ideas might grow into your first best-selling book someday!

ON THE WEB

MEET THE AUTHOR

Get acquainted with some of your favorite authors online at Web sites such as:

- Children's Book Council at http://www.cbcbooks.org/contacts
- Kids Reads at http://www.kidsreads.com/authors/authors.asp
- Society of Children's Book Writers and Illustrators at http://www.scbwi.org/links/mem_links.htm
- Yahoo Children's Authors at http://dir.yahoo.com/Arts/Humanities/Literature/Authors/Children_s

Or use an Internet search engine like http://www.google.com or http://www.yahooligans.com to find information about your favorite authors.

AT THE LIBRARY

BEHIND THE STORIES

Behind every bestselling book is an author with an interesting life story of their own to tell. Find out more about some of your favorite authors in books such as:

Ambrosek, Renee. *E.L. Konigsburg*. New York: Rosen, 2005.

Collins, David. *J.R.R. Tolkien*. Minneapolis, Minn.: Lerner, 2005.

Daniel, Susanna. *Lois Lowry*. New York: Rosen, 2003.

———. *Paul Zindel*. New York: Rosen, 2004.

Payment, Simone. *Scott O'Dell*. New York: Rosen, 2005.

Peterson, Todd. *Theodor Seuss Geisel: Author and Illustrator*. New York: Ferguson, 2006.

Primm, E. Russell. *Favorite Children's Authors and Illustrators (Five Volumes)*. Chanhassen, Minn.: Child's World, 2006.

Rosenburg, Aaron. *Madeleine L'Engle.* New York: Rosen, 2005.
Telford, Cee. *Judy Blume.* New York: Rosen, 2004.

WITH THE EXPERTS

Academy of American Poets
584 Broadway, Suite 604
New York, NY 10012-5243
http://www.poets.org

American Medical Writers Association
40 West Gude Drive, Suite 101
Rockville, MD 20850-1192
http://www.amwa.org

American Society of Journalists and Authors
1501 Broadway, Suite 302
New York, NY 10036-5505
http://www.asja.org

Author's Guild
31 East 32nd Street, 7th Floor
New York, NY 10016-5509
http://www.authorsguild.org

National Education Writers Association
2122 P Street NW, Suite 201
Washington, DC 20037-1037
http://www.ewa.org

Romance Writers of America
16000 Stuebner Airline Road, Suite 140
Spring, TX 77379-7389
http:/www.rwanational.org

Science Fiction and Fantasy Writers of America
PO Box 877
Chestertown, MD 21620
http://www.sfwa.org

Society of American Travel Writers
7044 South 13th Street
Oak Creek, WI 53154-1429
http://www.satw.org

Society of Children's Book Writers and Illustrators
8271 Beverly Boulevard
Los Angeles, CA 90048-4515
http://www.scbwi.org

GET ACQUAINTED

Paul and Sarah Edwards, Authors

CAREER PATH

CHILDHOOD ASPIRATION: Paul wanted to go into politics and to write a book. Sarah always wanted to write a book.

FIRST JOB: Sarah's first job was working at a city recreation center in a park. Paul's was delivering a downtown business newspaper.

CURRENT JOB: Authors; together they have written eight books.

DIFFERENT PATHS

Paul and Sarah Edwards both graduated from the University of Missouri. That's where they met and began their lifelong partnership. Paul "took his mother's advice" and went on to law school and became a lawyer. After graduation, Sarah thought she wanted to be a teacher. Her experiences as a student teacher changed her mind; she decided the teaching field was not for her. She worked for a short time at an insurance company. She then found what she says was a fabulous job with the Head Start program in Kansas City.

NO LONGER AN OPTION

Paul and Sarah got married. After giving birth to their son, Sarah found the long hours and busy travel schedule unfavorable while rearing a child. She returned to school, obtaining a master's degree in social work. This allowed her to open a private psychotherapy practice in her home.

FROM LAW INTO POLITICS

Meanwhile, Paul was practicing law and not enjoying it very much. He decided to enter the political arena. He served as coordinator of intergovernmental relations for a county. He then went to work as an urban specialist for a nonprofit agency. Another career change took him into political consulting (running other people's campaigns), which he did for several years.

A CHANGE OF FOCUS

The Edwardses were still searching for a way to do something in life that would be meaningful to both themselves and to others. The two of them started a business videotaping people in order to teach them how to present themselves. They were excellent trainers, but the void was still there. They resolved to find something that they could do together from home, that would be trendy, and that would help other people find their mission in life. That's how their first book came about.

IN THE RIGHT PLACE AT THE RIGHT TIME

During the early 1980s, more and more people were considering changes in careers. And many of those changes involved home-based careers or businesses. The Edwardses took advantage of the trend. They wrote and published their first book, *Working from Home* (it took five years to write and get published). It's now in its fifth edition. They also conducted workshops across the country, teaching people the basics of working from home.

PREACHING WHAT THEY PRACTICE

Authors of books that have sold over one and a half million copies, Paul and Sarah Edwards write, broadcast, and coach about new and better ways to live and work.

The Edwards's other works include *The Best Home Businesses for People 50+*, *The Best Home Businesses for the 21st Century*, *Changing Directions Without Losing Your Way*, *Cool*

Careers for Dummies, The Entrepreneurial Parent, Finding Your Perfect Work, Getting Business to Come to You, Home-Based Business for Dummies, Home Businesses You Can Buy, Making Money with Your Computer at Home, Secrets of Self-Employment, Teaming Up: The Small Business Guide to Collaborating with Others, The Practical Dreamers Handbook, Why Aren't You Your Own Boss?, and *Making Money in Cyberspace*. They, indeed, have become gurus for those who wish to learn about working from home successfully.

A HARD LESSON LEARNED

When the Edwardses first began searching for a publisher, they were assigned an editor who told them that they didn't write well. In response, they hired a writer who had written some 40 books. This writer was told by the same editor that he couldn't write either. The Edwardses then wrote an article for a major magazine and were told by the magazine editor that the writing was great. They then went back to the publishing house, met with someone else, got a new editor, and were on their way.

Rejection can take many forms and be difficult to accept, but it's an experience many writers will have. The Edwardses could have believed that first editor and just given up. But, they are really glad that they didn't. There will always be people who will try to hold you back. But there are many more who will give support and guidance. Seek those people out and persevere. Remember that it is worth taking a few knocks to follow your dream.

WRITE, WRITE, WRITE

The Edwardses' advice for would-be writers is to start writing at an early age. Keep a journal. Write about your experiences—things that you notice are different or funny. Record your observations. And an important part of writing (as painful as it might be) is to share your writing with others. Not everyone will like what you write, but you will be able to connect with some people. Get other people's perspectives. Find out if people are getting your message.

Book Producer

SKILL SET

- ✔ BUSINESS
- ✔ TALKING
- ✔ WRITING

SHORTCUTS

GO visit a bookstore and remember that every book on the shelves started with someone's idea.

READ books in all types of genres (categories). How about a biography, a mystery, or even a popular self-help book?

TRY making a list of all the different kinds of books you can think of—fiction and nonfiction.

WHAT IS A BOOK PRODUCER?

Book producers, or *packagers* as they are sometimes called, are a new breed of publishing professionals. Assuming some of the responsibilities of literary agent, writer, editor, designer, and printer, book producers take good ideas and turn them into marketable books. An especially unique feature about many book packagers is that instead of hiring full-time staffs, they put together "virtual" publishing teams that are tailor-made for specific projects. These "dream teams" tend to be small and versatile, with one person often assuming responsibility for more than one aspect of the project.

Book producers typically handle all, or most of, the steps of making books. They, or members of their team, may write and edit the book itself, design and illustrate the cover and pages, and prepare the materials for the printer. In addition, they must sell the concept to a publisher and negotiate the terms of the partnership. Sometimes they are also asked to develop strategies for marketing the book. Book producers tend to use the latest technology, which allows them to produce top-quality books quickly and efficiently.

The one thing that most books producers don't do that traditional publishers do is sell books. Instead, they sell the entire concept, or package, to publishers who handle all the marketing and distributing tasks. In order to succeed in this field, book packagers must know the kinds of books that specific publishers like and create projects that will enhance a publisher's list of books. Most book producers work with a variety of publishing houses, so the matchmaking can be quite a challenge.

The result can be a win-win situation for both the producer and the publisher. Publishers win by saving time and money over what it would take to manage and produce the same books in-house. Working with producers allows them to publish more titles in less time and with less effort than if they did it themselves. With so much of the time-consuming process of creating new books in other capable hands, the publishers can focus on building a solid list of books and devote their efforts to other aspects of the publishing process.

Book producers win in the same two ways: time and money. By turning the expensive and time-consuming marketing and distributing tasks over to publishing houses, they can focus their efforts on what they do best—producing books. By limiting their focus in this way, they are able to respond quickly to new trends and opportunities, which is a very good thing in the competitive world of publishing.

Because book producing is rather new, it isn't a field that requires a specific type of education or training. So far, book producers tend to be literary-minded entrepreneurs or people with experience in other aspects of the book industry. To prepare yourself for a career in this field, you'll want a strong background in one or more of the following areas: freelance writing or journalism, graphic design or commercial art, editing, or project management. After securing the necessary eduation, you might consider working for a traditional publisher to get a feel for the industry.

Although there are few guarantees in any profession, the future for book producers looks good. Multimedia and online projects are especially promising areas for talented book producers. Writers willing to ride the wave of the future may find some challenging opportunities in this profession.

TRY IT OUT

GO WITH WHAT YOU KNOW

Writers are often advised to write what they know. That means to write about subjects that are familiar and interesting to them. This isn't bad advice for book producers either.

What are you most interested in? Sports? Travel? Fashion? Food? Think of some of your favorite interests and come up with several ideas for books that you'd enjoy reading. Make a list of your ideas. When you've come up with a dozen or more ideas, visit the library or a big bookstore and see if there are similar books like the ones you have in mind. If you find similar books, think of ways to give yours a different twist.

ABCS OF BOOK PRODUCING

Pretend that you are a book producer and have just landed a big contract to produce an ABC book for preschoolers. Before you get started, take a look at the competition. Either go to the library and ask the librarian to direct you to a variety of alphabet books or go online to Amazon (http://www.amazon.com) or Barnes and Noble (http://www.bn.com) and use their search engines to look for *ABC books*. Notice all the creative ways authors have used to teach children the alphabet. Come up with a fun theme of your own and use simple words to introduce each letter of the alphabet on a separate sheet of paper. Find pictures in magazines and online to illustrate each page, and put all your pages together into a book with an eye-catching cover and really imaginative title.

You can find ideas for making homemade books at http://familycrafts.about.com/od/homemadebooks.

ON THE WEB

HOW BOOKS GET MADE

There are lots of steps involved in making books and book producers are usually involved in them all. Find out more about how books are made at some of these online resources:

- Aliki the author cat introduces the basic steps of making a book at http://www.harperchildrens.com/hch/picture/features/aliki/howabook/book1.asp.
- Puffin tells all about the book-making process at http://www.penguin.com.au/PUFFIN/kids/book/f_book.htm.
- See a book being created page by page at http://www.collectionscanada.ca/pagebypage.
- Make your own books with instructions found at http://library.thinkquest.org/J001156/bookmade.htm.
- Take an online tour of a book manufacturing facility at http://www.tshore.com/AboutUs/BookManufacturingTour/tabid/63/Default.aspx and http://www.friesens.com/Bookplant/PlantTour/BPTour.asp.

MEET THE PRODUCERS

Go online to visit the Web sites of some of these producers to get a better sense of the kinds of books they create:

- Becker & Mayer at http://beckermayer.com
- Bright Futures Press at http://www.brightfuturespress.com
- Parachute Publishing at http://www.parachutepublishing.com
- Quirk Packaging at http://quirkpackaging.com
- Shoreline Publishing at http://shorelinepublishing.com

AT THE LIBRARY

DO SOME COMPARISON SHOPPING

Find some of these kid-friendly books that are listed below:

John Deere: Big Building Site, Little Building Site. New York: DK Publishing, 2006.

Buckley, James, Jr., and Robert Stremme. *Scholastic Book of Lists New and Updated*. New York: Scholastic, 2006.

DK Publishing. *Baseball*. New York: DK Publishing, 2005.

Kurtti, Jeff. *Disney Villains: The Top Secret Files*. New York: Disney Books, 2005.

Here are a couple titles from series to look for:

Rotten School, written by R.L. Stine (New York: Harper Collins, 2006) and produced by Parachute Publishing.

Virtual Apprentice: Author, written by Gail Karlitz (New York: Ferguson, 2007) and produced by Bright Futures Press.

Welcome to the U.S.A., edited by E. Russell Primm III (Chanhassen, Minn.: Child's World, 2005) and produced by Editorial Directions.

WITH THE EXPERTS

American Book Producers Association
381 Park Avenue South
New York, NY 10010-8806
http://www.abpaonline.org

Small Publishers Association of North America
1618 West Colorado Avenue
Colorado Springs, CO 80904-4029
http://www.spannet.org

GET ACQUAINTED

Susan Lingo, Book Packager

CAREER PATH

CHILDHOOD ASPIRATION: To be a storm-chaser tracking down tornadoes.

FIRST JOB: Worked as a clerk in a health food store.

CURRENT JOB: Author, publisher, and owner of Bright Ideas Books.

A STRANGE THING HAPPENED ON THE WAY TO THE CLASSROOM

Susan Lingo actually started her professional career as a teacher. In fact, she has taught every grade except fifth grade. Several years ago, when her family moved to a new state, Lingo couldn't find a teaching position. She decided the time was right to follow the advice of some of her fellow teachers and write a book about her ideas for making learning fun.

Lingo had so many ideas that she thought the best approach might be to write a magazine for teachers. That way she could introduce new ideas every month. She put together a proposal and sent it to a publisher. The publisher rejected the magazine concept but liked her ideas so much that she was asked to do 14 books instead. Obviously, Lingo's career as an author was launched in a big way. Today, Lingo has 84 books (and counting) to her credit.

ONE THING LEADS TO ANOTHER

Writing all those books put Lingo in contact with lots of publishing houses. They began to know and respect her work. One publisher liked her work so much that she offered Lingo a job as the editor of her children's book division. Lingo accepted the position on the condition that she could keep on writing her own books.

As it turns out, the experience (like most big experiences in life) had its pros and cons. On the good side was the opportunity to learn the fine points of publishing and be part of the process from beginning to end. For Lingo, the downside of the job was the editing. Instead of working in the creative realm of her own ideas, she ended up fixing other people's mistakes. She found the role of manuscript mender to be very frustrating and eventually decided to stick with what she does best—writing her own books.

MOVING ON DOWN THE ROAD

This time Lingo decided to blend her writing experience with her publishing experience and actually produce her books for publishers. This way she retains complete creative control of the project from start to finish and can make it happen the way she sees fit. Lingo still writes the manuscripts and comes up with the overall concept of how the book should look. Then she hires designers and editors to do the rest. Sometimes Lingo even designs the covers and pages of her books herself.

As Lingo continues to crank out books, she's found the following six steps to be key to her success as a book producer.

1. Recognize a need for a book and respond to that need with a good idea.

2. Write an outline that is complete enough that someone else can understand what the book would be about.
3. Prepare a proposal and sample chapters.
4. Match the book idea with a publishing house that does similar books.
5. Make the pitch and close the deal.
6. Deliver such a great product that publishers come back for more.

BEYOND ONCE UPON A TIME

Lingo echoes the sentiment that book producers should "go with what they know." She says it would have been impossible for her to write and produce the learning activity books that she focuses on if it hadn't been for her classroom experience as a teacher.

She says that if you want to produce books, you need to start with books that you find interesting. Lingo also says that the most important skill you'll need to develop as a writer is self-discipline. The books won't write themselves!

Bookseller

SKILL SET

- ✔ BUSINESS
- ✔ TALKING
- ✔ WRITING

SHORTCUTS

GO compare one of the book superstore chains with a privately owned bookstore.

READ the latest *Booksense* bestseller lists online at http://www.bookweb.org.

TRY volunteering at your school's book fair (or talk to the school librarian about hosting one).

WHAT IS A BOOKSELLER?

First, a clarification: There really isn't a particular career called bookseller. Instead, there are several different ways to make a living selling books. Such careers are explained in the following pages.

Bookstore owners enjoy the dream job of many a book lover. Running their own business, surrounded by good books and other literary fans, is the perfect combination for a fun job. At its best it can be fun, stimulating, and profitable. Competition from the gigantic bookstore chains, however, has made it more challenging for independent bookstore owners. Those who succeed tend to do so by carving out a unique niche. Whether it's with mysteries, children's books, audio books, educational materials, or CD-ROM products, small bookstores can offer what the big guys can't in terms of specialized service and expertise and, quite often, in a fun environment to indulge one's fancy for a particular genre.

Bookstore managers keep things running smoothly in larger bookstores and bookstore chains. They do this in much the same way that any business manager would, by handling administrative tasks such as hiring and scheduling staff, keeping track of inventory, and providing customer service.

Book buyers are the people who decide which of the thousands of new books published each year get space on the bookstore shelves. Buyers may work for the corporate headquarters of one of the major chains, a larger independent bookstore, a school district, or a university. Their job is to keep the shelves stocked with books readers will want to buy. Buyers must stay current with what's hot and new in publishing by meeting with publisher's representatives, attending trade shows, and reading lots of catalogs and industry publications. The tricky part is making educated guesses about how well each book will sell, being prepared for overnight sensations (as a guest appearance on a television talk show might spark), and staying one step ahead of the latest trends and fads. Look at the sale table in any bookstore to find evidence of bad calls by book buyers and overzealous publishers.

Publisher's representatives are employed by a specific publishing house or work independently for any number of companies. Their job is to introduce books to book buyers. A representative is generally responsible for a specific and sometimes sizable region, called a territory, so they often spend a good deal of time traveling around to the places where books are sold—bookstores, school districts, universities, and trade shows. Equal parts of salesmanship and marketing savvy are required to do this job well.

Many of these career ideas lend themselves to on-the-job learning opportunities or even official apprenticeships. Working in a bookstore is a good first step toward any of these options. Higher-level positions such as book buyer may require training or experience in business or marketing as well. In addition, some publishers look for expertise in a specific area. This is especially true for working with educational or academic books, where many reps are experienced teachers.

For someone who loves good writing and has an interest in business, a career in book sales can be a great choice.

TAKE A TRIP!

Bookseller

BOOK EXCHANGE

You don't have to be grown up and have lots of money to run your own bookstore. All you need are a few friends who like to read and are willing to trade some books from their own collections. To participate, ask everybody to bring a couple of books to share. Give each person a certain amount of credit for every book that they bring. You might designate the credit with index cards, bookmarks, or even play money from a board game. You'll want to make rules about things such as whether a hardcover book is worth more than a paperback and so forth.

Arrange a special time and place for everyone to get together and use their credit to "buy" books. For a special touch (and extra fun), you might want to serve refreshments, play some music, or otherwise set the tone for a lively literary experience.

THE TOP SELLERS

Find a current list of best-selling books. Your library, a bookstore, or the book section of the Sunday newspaper will list them. Or go online to look at the *New York Times Book Review* at http://www.nytimes.com/pages/books/index.html.

Pick a book and follow its progress for a couple of weeks to see how it does. Also, whenever possible or appropriate, read some of the best sellers on the children's list to see what all the fuss is about. As you read, try to imagine why that particular book made it to the top. What makes it so special?

ON THE WEB

ONLINE WINDOW SHOPPING

Thanks to the Internet, you no longer have to live in a big city to have access to the best bookstores. Go online to find all kinds of specialty bookstores all over the world at http://www.bookwire.com or visit some of these online super bookstores:

- Amazon at http://www.amazon.com
- Barnes and Noble at http://www.bn.com
- Books-a-Million at http://www.booksamillion.com
- Borders at http://www.borders.com
- Tattered Cover at http://www.tatteredcover.com

While you are there, compare how easy it is to find what you are looking for at each site. Make a list from one to five and rank the Web sites with the most user-friendly one being number one and the least being five.

AND THE WINNER IS...

There are the best sellers, and there are the award winners. Sometimes you'll find the same books on both lists, but sometimes you won't. Remember, best seller doesn't necessarily mean the best read. Find out about some of the most prestigious children's book awards and the winners at the following Web sites:

- Newbery Medal, for the author of the most distinguished contribution to American literature for children, at http://www.ala.org/alsc/newbery.html
- Caldecott Award, for the artist of the most distinguished American picture book for children, at http://www.ala.org/alsc/caldecott.html
- Coretta Scott King Award, for most outstanding contribution by an African-American author or illustrator, at http://www.ala.org/ala/emiert/corettascottking bookaward/corettascott.htm

AT THE LIBRARY

BLOCKBUSTER BOOKS

Speaking of award-winning books, see if you can tell why some of the following books were selected as the "cream of the crop" in children's books:

Choldenko, Gennifer. *Al Capone Does My Shirts*. New York: Putnam, 2006.

DiCamillo, Kate. *Because of Winn-Dixie*. Cambridge, Mass.: Candlewick, 2001.

Gerstein, Mordicai. *The Man Who Walked Between the Towers*. Minneapolis, Minn.: Millbrook Press, 2004.

Hiaasen, Carl. *Hoot*. New York: Knopf, 2003.

Levine, Gail Carson. *Ella Enchanted*. New York: Harper Collins, 1998.

Juster, Norton, and Chris Raschka. *The Hello, Goodbye Window*. New York: Scholastic, 2005.

Also, ask your school or public librarian for other suggestions. Warning: Good books can be addicting!

WITH THE EXPERTS

American Booksellers Association
200 White Plains Road
Tarrytown, NY 10591-5808
http://www.bookweb.org and
http://www.booksense.com

National Association of Publishers' Representatives
54 Cove Road
Huntington, NY 11743-2252
http://www.naprassoc.com

GET ACQUAINTED

Clara Villarosa, Bookstore Owner

CAREER PATH

CHILDHOOD ASPIRATION: To be a teacher.

FIRST JOB: Working for a seamstress.

CURRENT JOB: Owner of Hue-Man Bookstore and Cafe, an African-American bookstore in Harlem.

A NEW DIRECTION

Clara Villarosa had always wanted to be a teacher and started college with that goal in mind. After a while, she discovered that there was more to the education field than teaching. She changed her college major and went on to earn a master's degree in social work. She began her career as a psychiatric social worker in a mental health clinic.

FULL-TIME MOM

While her children were young, Villarosa worked outside the home one day a week and spent the rest of her time being a full-time mother. When her youngest child entered school, Villarosa worked part time. Then the family moved from Chicago to Denver, and Villarosa went to work at Children's Hospital as chief psychiatric social worker in the department of behavioral sciences. After working at the hospital for a number of years, she advanced to assistant hospital administrator.

BACK TO SCHOOL

When Villarosa's children were in college, she decided to join the party and went back to school too. She started working toward a doctorate (a Ph.D.) in social work. As happens to a lot of students, she ran out of money before she finished the program. Oh well! On to the next stage of her life!

INTO THE BUSINESS WORLD

The next stop on Villarosa's career journey took her to a major bank. Her management skills led her all the way up to a position as assistant vice president of human resources and strategic planning. Meanwhile, though, she had this idea in the back of her mind: She wanted to own her own bookstore. So while she was working at the bank, Villarosa started saving money. Eventually she'd saved enough, along with the help of two partners, to open a very small version of her dream bookstore. The Denver-based store continued to succeed over the years and eventually became the largest African-American bookstore in the country.

The store specialized in African-American and African books with sections of fiction, history, children's, and religious books. It had a large selection of magazines, greeting cards, unique gifts, and fine art prints.

A CHANGE OF PLANS

After 16 years in the business, Villarosa decided to retire and relocate to New York City where her two daughters and two young grandchildren lived. After all, she was 70 years old and it was time to just enjoy family for a while.

As it turns out, she met a real estate developer who nudged her into changing those plans a bit. He was looking for a bookstore to join a commercial project he was building in Harlem, an ethnically diverse community in New York City. A bookstore like Hue-Man would be a perfect fit for the neighborhood, he said, and soon—quite unexpectedly—Villarosa found herself opening a new state-of-the-art bookstore there. Villarosa compares the experiences of owning stores in Denver and New York City in this way, "In Denver, I was a big fish in a small pond, but in New York I was a small fish in a big pond."

Nonetheless, with half a million potential customers in New York City's African-American community compared to just 100,000 in Denver, the new store was a huge success. The store became such an important part of the community that former U.S. president Bill Clinton, whose office is just two blocks away from the store, chose Hue-man to host a book signing when his memoir, *My Life*, was released. Villarosa recalls that his visit was a very big day, complete with Secret Service agents, security checkpoints, and thousands of customers. She says they sold 2,119 copies of his book that day and that Clinton graciously stayed to sign every single copy.

KEYS TO SUCCESS

Villarosa believes it is critical for young people to have a love of reading. So much of education is based on reading. She says to start reading early and develop a real appreciation for books and learning. Two other skills important in any walk of life are speaking skills and writing skills. She puts it very simply: read, write, and speak well.

In 2004, Villarosa turned the day-to-day operations of the bookstore over to a managing partner and is finally starting to enjoy her retirement. Now she has plenty of time to devote to encourage her grandchildren to cultivate good reading skills. She says that she asks Kali (age 10) and Nic (age 7) to read at least one book a week and write a paragraph describing what the book was about. Then when Grandma comes to visit, the children tell her about what they've read. Each time they complete this process, Grandma rewards them with a silver dollar. Of course, her granddaughter talked her into upping the ante a bit when she completed one of the 500+ page titles in the Harry Potter series!

Corporate Communicator

SKILL SET

- ✔ BUSINESS
- ✔ TALKING
- ✔ WRITING

SHORTCUTS

GO to the library and ask to see some of the annual reports submitted by local businesses.

READ the business section of the newspaper and look for quotes by company spokespeople.

TRY visiting the Web site of a favorite company.

WHAT IS A CORPORATE COMMUNICATOR?

Getting the word out about a company in a way that builds a positive image is the main function of a corporate communicator. Corporate communicators use their top-notch verbal and written communication skills to convey carefully crafted messages about the company they represent. To do so, the job may include working with the media and other sources to reach an external audience (that is, all the people who are touched by the company, from the neighbors who live near the place of business to its paying customers). Likewise, corporate communicators also need to effectively stay in touch with internal audiences (the company's employees). This is especially important in large corporations that may employ thousands of people in dozens of locations.

Some of the tools that corporate communicators use to reach these audiences include press releases, newsletters, brochures, annual reports, multimedia presentations, and bulletin board displays. Technology has added some new tools to the list in the form of some fairly sophisticated telephone or computer e-mail information systems. It is estimated that businesses spend a combined total of around $1 billion on internal communication activities alone, so you can imagine that there is plenty of work to do in this profession.

Corporate communicators go by many job titles including public relations specialist, corporate communications director, community affairs coordinator, communications specialist, press secretary, public information officer, and spokesperson. Corporate communicators often specialize in a particular area within the company. Specialties within the profession include

community relations, which involves developing activities that allow a business to give something back to the community where the business operates. This area might include special events, volunteer programs, and charitable giving projects.

government relations, which involves monitoring and influencing legislation that affects the company.

investor relations, which involves keeping investors informed about the company and its financial status. Preparing annual reports and coordinating shareholder meetings are part of the job.

corporate training, which involves providing in-house workshops and training sessions about topics such as communication skills, diversity, and gender equity.

A college degree is essential for corporate communicators. Majors in areas such as communications, public relations, business, or marketing are good educational choices for those interested in this line of work. Fluency in a foreign language is considered a plus in today's global economy.

There are three ways to boost your chances for landing a good job in this field. One way is to get involved in community volunteer programs. Another is to take advantage of every work-study, cooperative education, or internship opportunity that comes your way in order to gain some real work experience. The third is to spend time working or living in another culture, perhaps as an exchange student or Peace Corps volunteer. Surround yourself with people who speak another language, and your communication skills are guaranteed to improve!

WHAT IF

Corporate communicators have to be prepared for anything. In fact, these professionals are often asked to prepare step-by-step plans for handling potential crises, such as an earthquake or an injury resulting from the use of the company's products. These plans provide scripts and action plans so that everyone knows exactly what to do in case, heaven forbid, something bad happens.

Pretend that you are the person in charge of handling public relations for your school. Here are a couple of scenarios for you to consider. Make a plan to come through these mini-disasters with as little trouble as possible. Each plan should have at least five steps.

- A bus breaks down on the way to school during a snowstorm.
- The cafeteria runs out of food before everyone is served.
- Half of the teachers don't show up for school one day.

CORPORATE IMAGE

Corporations use logos, distinct graphic images, to build their brand or image. Logos give consumers a "picture" that helps them instantly connect an image with a specific company. It's a communications tool that helps companies stand out from the rest of the crowd.

Do they work? Let's check. What company comes to mind when you see golden arches? What company do you think about when you hear the words "just do it" and see a swish symbol? If you answered McDonald's and Nike, you just proved that logos work.

So, pretend that your name is the name of an up and coming corporation. Use markers, crayons, or colored pencils to create an interesting logo using the letters of your first or last name.

THE SPIN DOCTOR IS IN

Corporate communicators must learn quickly how to make the most of a bad situation. Their job is to put a positive spin on a bad situation; however their job is not to lie or deceive. Honesty is the name of this game. Only a fool would try to get away with lying to the public.

Suppose your school has decided to add an extra hour to the end of every school day. The principal is concerned that the students and staff might not receive this news very well. She asks you to come up with a plan for presenting the news in a way that will make the idea more agreeable to everyone.

What would you do? First, come up with some good reasons and then develop promotional materials such as posters and special events that might help soften the news.

ON THE WEB

THE INTERNET MARKETPLACE

It probably won't surprise you that Web sites are becoming a very popular means for businesses to communicate with their audiences. Take a look at some of these popular sites and see how they do it:

http://www.adidas.com
http://www.levi.com

http://www.nike.com
http://www.revlon.com
http://www.sony.com

 AT THE LIBRARY

CORPORATE ROLE MODELS

Read about some of America's most prominent corporate leaders—past and present—in book such as:

Bemmer, Rod, with Tracey Nelsen Maurer. *John Deere*. St. Paul, Minn.: MBI Publishing, 2006.
Krohn, Katherine E. *Just the Facts Biography: Oprah Winfrey*. Minneapolis, Minn.: Lerner, 2004.
Lesinski, Jeanne. *Bill Gates*. Minneapolis, Minn.: Lerner, 2005.
McLuskey, Krista. *Women in Profile: Entrepreneurs*. New York: Crabtree, 1999.
Meachem, Dana. *Andrew Carnegie: Captain of Industry*. Mankato, Minn.: Capstone, 2005.
O'Hearn, Michael. *Henry Ford and the Model T*. Mankato, Minn.: Capstone, 2006.
Ryan, Bernard, Jr. *Jeff Bezos: Business Executive and Founder of Amazon.com*. New York: Ferguson, 2005.

WITH THE EXPERTS

Association for Business Communication
PO Box 6143
Nacogdoches, TX 75962-0001
http://www.businesscommunication.org

Association for Women in Communications
3337 Duke Street
Alexandria, VA 22314-5219
http://www.womcom.org

International Association of Business Communicators
One Hallidie Plaza, Suite 600
San Francisco, CA 94102-2842
http://www.iabc.com

Public Relations Society of America
33 Maiden Lane, 11th Floor
New York, NY 10038-5150
http://www.prsa.org

GET ACQUAINTED

Chris Chavez, Corporate Communicator

CAREER PATH

CHILDHOOD ASPIRATION: To be a pro-football quarterback.

FIRST JOB: Washing pizza pans at Godfather's Pizza.

CURRENT JOB: Senior manager of community relations for Qwest Foundation.

OUT OF THE QUESTION

Chris Chavez really wanted to be a pro-football quarterback, but when he stopped growing at the not-so-menacing height of five feet eight, he decided he should probably pursue another career. He grew up in Laramie, Wyoming, where his mother was a Spanish teacher and his father, a conductor for the Union Pacific railroad. He attended schools in Laramie and excelled academically in high school. College was the logical next step.

A PROUD MOMENT

Chavez is very proud of the fact that he is the first male member on either his mother's or his father's side of the family to go to college. He was accepted at both Stanford University and Notre Dame, but the necessary financial support was not available for him to attend. He received a full scholarship to the University of Wyoming, where he majored in journalism.

EENY, MEENY, MINEY, MO

After graduation, Chavez was offered two jobs. One was a position as assistant press secretary for then-Congressman Dick Cheney (Wyoming). The other job offer came from Jackson Hole, Wyoming. The job was outdoors editor for the *Jackson Hole Guide* (which at that time was the top weekly newspaper in the country).

Chavez took the job in Jackson Hole. He needed a break after four hard years of college. Through his job he was able to enjoy and simultaneously write about downhill skiing, fly fishing, kayaking, canoeing on the Snake River, and climbing the Teton Mountains. He won five state awards for news, feature, and column writing. He worked at the paper for two and a half years.

GIVE THE CORPORATE WORLD A TRY

Next Chavez decided to try his hand at corporate public relations. He was hired by the Martin-Marietta Astronautics Group (the company that designs components for the space program). He went to work as public relations manager. He was thrilled to be working for a major corporation, making a good salary, and able to spend money on himself. Unfortunately, he was laid off nine months later when government contracts were cut. It was time to look for another job, so he hit the streets again.

A COMMUNITY FOCUS

Chavez was fortunate to land a job as public relations director for Downtown Denver Partnership, a private, nonprofit promotional agency for downtown Denver, Colorado. He says it was a wonderful job. During his years there, Chavez promoted notable events such as the pope's visit to Colorado, and the opening of Coors Baseball Field, a new downtown library, and an amusement park. Downtown Denver was coming into its own, and Chavez was right in the middle of it. He worked with the media and wrote speeches, brochures, and annual reports.

CORPORATE WORK WITH A COMMUNITY TWIST

After five years, Chavez started thinking about a career change and moving on to other challenges. He was going through some other life changes as well, including getting married. When Chavez returned from his honeymoon, he received a call from an executive recruiter asking him if he was interested in a new job. One month later, he was hired by Qwest Communications. He is now in charge of the company's community relations for 14 states.

Chavez handles community outreach and events, works with the media, is the liaison and representative in the western section of the country for the Qwest Foundation, and administers Foundation funds. He also handles employee volunteer programs and spends a lot of time reviewing proposals from groups wanting money for various programs.

SOME PROFESSIONAL ADVICE

Chavez believes that one of the most important things for a young person to do is to identify a mentor or a role model—someone you look up to and want to be like. Talk to them or write to them; ask them how they got where they are. It's important to have someone to identify with and to ask for advice.

GOOD WRITERS ARE GOOD READERS

If you want to go into the writing field, it is critical that you be a good reader. Chavez advises reading at least one book a month and one or two newspapers a day. Keep up on current events, study how people write, and most importantly, do your own writing.

Keep a journal (keep it private if you don't want anyone to read it), and practice sentence structure. Be creative, and keep your mind open to what's going on in the world! There are always opportunities for those who look hard enough.

Editor

SKILL SET

- ✔ COMPUTERS
- ✔ TALKING
- ✔ WRITING

SHORTCUTS

GO tour a large print shop to find out how books are produced.

READ a favorite magazine and look at the masthead, which lists many of the people it took to put the issue together. You'll discover that publishing is a team effort!

TRY helping your English teacher edit student essays. See how many grammatical errors you can find and fix.

WHAT IS AN EDITOR?

Editors make sure that the books, magazines, newspapers, and other publications that you read provide correct information and are written clearly and grammatically. A good word to describe an editor's role in the publishing process is liaison, or go-between. In one sense, an editor is the liaison between a book's author and its readers. The job here is to do everything possible to assure the best quality of work for the reader's enjoyment. The editor works with an author throughout the writing process to help shape a writer's ideas into content suitable for publication.

In another sense, an editor acts as liaison for the publisher, acquiring new books and negotiating contracts that are mutually beneficial for the authors and the publisher. This part of the process can be as mundane as digging through the "slush piles," or stacks of unsolicited manuscripts, that are found in every editor's office—although this is where editors sometimes find the perfect new book to add to the publisher's list—to as glamorous as having lunch with a best-selling author to discuss ideas for his or her next book.

Another way that editors act as liaison is with the production staff. In production, manuscripts become books, and the process involves artists, page designers, and printers. An editor must maintain a clear vision of the "identity" of each book in order to guide the creative team in producing a look that is suitable.

Finally, the editor typically serves as go-between with the marketing department. It won't matter how well the book is written and how nicely it's designed if there isn't a solid plan for getting the book into the hands of readers. It all comes down to selling books, and the editor is often one of the best resources for helping this process move in the right direction.

In short, editors have to be good jugglers because they are responsible for many aspects of the publishing process. It's a lot to do for one book, but imagine what's it like to be responsible for dozens of books in various stages of development. It can be demanding but very exciting work.

Fortunately, in many publishing houses, the various tasks of an editor are shared by more than one person. In fact, in larger houses, there are specific types of editors who are responsible for specific parts of the editorial process. Following are descriptions of the different types of editors.

Editorial assistants handle the nitty-gritty details of the editorial office in a manner similar to a clerk or secretary. However, due to the nature of their work and proximity to more experienced professionals, they are often being primed for bigger and better things within the publishing house.

Assistant editors help sort through the sometimes massive slush piles, screening manuscripts, responding to queries from authors, and assisting in other ways.

Associate editors assume similar duties as assistant editors but have more responsibility for managing projects from beginning to end.

Editors handle many of the same aspects of a project as associate editors, but full-fledged editors tend to work on more important books. In addition to working with authors and agents to acquire books from submitted manuscripts, editors may also come up with their own project ideas and manage all the processes of turning the ideas into books.

Senior editors manage other editors and work on major projects. Senior editors also handle more of the administrative aspects of the process such as long-range plans, budgets, and sales projections. In smaller publishing companies, the senior editor assumes much of the responsibility for acquiring new books as well.

Acquisitions editors are constantly on the lookout for good books to add to their publisher's list. They read many manuscript submissions and proposals, conduct research on the book's marketability, and select projects that will enhance their list. Knowing the audience and understanding what it wants to read are crucial elements for the success of an acquisitions editor.

Copy editors are among the last people to read a manuscript or other publication before it goes to print. They correct the facts, continuity, grammar, sentence structure, and spelling, and they make sure that everything is absolutely perfect before the manuscript goes to print.

Publishers tend to hire editors with college degrees in areas such as liberal arts, English, and communications. Even with a college degree, most editors start at the bottom of the editorial career ladder as editorial assistants. However, with hard work, talent, and initiative, an editor might expect to start moving up that ladder rather quickly.

GET YOUR ACT TOGETHER

Great organizational skills are the one trait that all successful editors share. After all, they are often responsible for managing several (or many!) book projects at the same time. To make sure that no details or deadlines fall through the cracks, editors rely on a variety of planning tools and timelines to keep themselves on track. Next time you have a paper or other big assignment due, take some time to think through all the steps involved, list the due dates, and make a chart to keep yourself on top of everything.

GIVE YOUR TEXTBOOK A MAKEOVER

Go to your locker and pull out your least favorite textbook. Thumb through the textbook, and make a list of the things you don't like about it. The fact that it's a math book and you hate math isn't exactly what you are after; rather, think about those elements that make it hard or unpleasant to read.

After you've identified its bad points, make a list of the elements that you like. Perhaps the use of color livens things up or the sidebars, maps, or tables that are included with each chapter are easy to understand.

Finally, pretend that you are the editor at a textbook publishing house and have been asked to update this textbook for a new edition. Write a letter to your publisher describing the ways you think the book could be improved to better meet the needs of its intended audience. Perhaps include a sample revised page or a photocopy of a page on which you have edited and updated.

✓ CHECK IT OUT

ON THE WEB

THE CYBER-EDITOR

Get ready to impress your teachers (and yourself) with your extraordinary editing skills with a little help from the fun and games found at some of the Web sites below.

- Let Shakespeare show you how the editing process affects an author's words from pen to print and from stage to screen at http://www.ciconline.org/bdp1.
- Practice your proofreading skills at http://eduplace.com/kids/hme/k_5/proofread.
- Learn the ABCs of writing at http://www.angelfire.com/wi/writingprocess.
- Brush up on your grammar skills at http://www.eduplace.com/kids/hme/k_5/quizzes.
- Go bananas with the Grammar Gorillas at http://www.funbrain.com/grammar.

READ WHAT EDITORS READ

The following resources will keep you current on what's happening in the publishing industry and introduce you to some of the people and publishers that might become your future employers. Check out their very informative Web sites:

- Association of American Publishers at http://www.publishers.org
- Publishers Marketplace at http://www.publishersmarketplace.com
- Publishers Weekly at http://www.publishersweekly.com

Get the latest news in children's books!

AT THE LIBRARY

GOT GRAMMAR?

When it comes to grammar, good editors have it down. They know their adjectives from their adverbs and it's their job to make sure that their authors do too. Here are some books to help you brush up your own skills.

Block, Cheryl. *Editor In Chief: A2*. Seaside, Calif.: Critical Thinking Co., 2000.

———. *Editor In Chief: B2*. Seaside, Calif.: Critical Thinking Co., 2002.

———. *Editor In Chief: C2*. Seaside, Calif.: Critical Thinking Co., 2001.

———. *Language Mechanic: Tuning Up English With Logic*. Seaside, Calif.: Critical Thinking Co., 2000.

Also, check out the amusing *Words are CATegorical* series by Brian P. Cleary (Minneapolis, Minn.: Lerner). There are separate volumes for nouns, adverbs, adjectives, and other parts of speech, all with attention-getting titles like *Dearly, Nearly, Insincerely: What is an Adverb*? and *Hairy, Scary, Ordinary: What is an Adjective*?

WITH THE EXPERTS

American Society of Newspaper Editors
11690-B Sunrise Valley Drive
Reston, VA 20191-1409
http://www.asne.org

Association of American Publishers
71 Fifth Avenue, 2nd Floor
New York, NY 10003-3004
http://www.publishers.org

Editorial Freelancers Association
71 West 23rd Street, Suite 1910
New York, NY 10010-4181
http://www.the-efa.org

Magazine Publishers of America
810 Seventh Avenue, 24th Floor
New York, NY 10019-5873
http://www.magazine.org

Society of American Business Editors and Writers
Missouri School of Journalism
385 McReynolds
Columbia, MO 65211-1200
http://www.sabew.org

GET ACQUAINTED

Eileen O'Reilly, Online Editor

CAREER PATH

CHILDHOOD ASPIRATION: To be a reporter or talk show host.

FIRST JOB: Scooping ice cream at Baskin-Robbins.

CURRENT JOB: Online editor for Monster.com.

A MULTIMEDIA CAREER

During the course of Eileen O'Reilly's career, she has had the opportunity to work with words in several different types of media. O'Reilly majored in political science at the University of Colorado at Boulder; after graduation, she headed east to New York City, America's "media center."

She got her start working in production for *House and Garden* magazine. Since this magazine happens to be published by one of the biggest names in the business, Condé Nast, O'Reilly found plenty of opportunity to move up the ranks in this company. She eventually made her way to a senior editorial position after learning the ropes at magazines such as *Glamour*, *Vanity Fair*, *Traveler*, and *Self*.

After working several years on magazines, O'Reilly decided to change mediums, turning to television shows. Working on various projects for PBS (the Public Broadcasting System) and local affiliates, she discovered a whole new dimension in editing. Instead of working primarily with words and pictures at a desk, this job took her all over the city researching and filming segments.

Next stop on the career path was a job with a publisher of interactive CD-ROM products. Once again, O'Reilly found herself faced with the challenge of learning a completely new way of communicating information. Putting together the content for a project focusing on American Sign Language involved incredible organization skills and attention to details. The pace was completely different from her work in television, as she found that just one project could consume more than a year of intense effort.

A NEW FRONTIER

Next on O'Reilly's resume was a stint as producer of the Student Center, a career and job search Web site that helped students find out about different careers, research specific companies, and prepare resumes for their first venture out into the workplace. O'Reilly was initially amazed at the constant flow of information and, after working at magazines where issues were prepared with three months lead time, had to get used to the fast pace of the online environment. But, she admits, it was really exciting to be there at the very beginning to help figure out how to make the most of the new online technologies.

Later, this Web site was bought out by Monster.com, a large online job-hunting resource for people of all ages. There O'Reilly encountered exciting new challenges working with a growing, and very successful, high-tech company.

A TURNING POINT

O'Reilly says that it was a college internship that got her interested in a career in communications. She worked for a public relations firm and had the chance to be involved in projects involving famous sports figures, a fashion magazine, and sports events. It was here that she discovered what having a real job was really like. She learned how to dress for an office job, arrive on time for work, and work as part of a creative team.

THE PEOPLE MAKE THE DIFFERENCE

One of the best parts of working in the media is the people. O'Reilly says that she especially enjoys working with the bright, interesting people she's found everywhere in this profession.

In addition, O'Reilly has found that networking with others in the profession has been the key to some of the really exciting opportunities that have come her way. Quite often, meeting someone who knows someone else who was doing something interesting led to O'Reilly's new jobs. She's also had the opportunity to learn from watching others succeed in the business. One of the perks of her current job is helping the women who founded the company forge new ground in this exciting new field of communication.

Freelance Writer

SKILL SET

- ✔ ADVENTURE
- ✔ BUSINESS
- ✔ WRITING

SHORTCUTS

GO visit the place where your local newspaper is published.

READ *The Elements of Style Illustrated* by William Strunk Jr. and E.B. White (New York: Penguin, 2005).

TRY writing an article for your school newspaper.

WHAT IS A FREELANCE WRITER?

Freelance writers are writers for hire. They aren't actually employed by a specific company; instead, they work on various projects from a variety of sources. In a sense, they run their own businesses with their writing skills being the product offered for sale.

Freelance writers find that potential clients are everywhere. Virtually every magazine found on supermarket

shelves is filled with submissions from freelance writers. Newspapers often run feature stories written by freelance writers. Textbooks, encyclopedias, and other reference books are commonly filled with the work of freelance writers. In addition, some publishers hire writers to work on books for a specific project under development.

Two other lucrative areas for freelancers are business writing and technical writing. Businesses of all kinds and sizes often hire freelance writers to work on projects such as proposals, speeches, annual reports, newsletters, brochures, and other publications. Some freelance writers work exclusively for public relations firms; advertising agencies, in particular, will use experienced writers to help with various projects. This way the agency handles the marketing aspects of finding clients, and the writer focuses on pleasing the client with well-crafted written materials.

Technical writers are currently in big demand to translate software programs and other complicated documents into instructions that just about anyone can understand. Technical writing isn't for everyone. Sometimes the work requires a writer to have very specialized technical knowledge as well as top-notch writing skills.

Although the pay isn't always quite as good, some freelance writers specialize in working with nonprofit organizations and charities. The ability to write clear and convincing grant proposals is a hot commodity among agencies that depend on funds from foundations and benevolent corporations for their support.

Instead of receiving a salary like an employee or royalties like an author, freelancers are generally paid a flat fee. There is a big gap between low-end and top-end fees: some projects pay as little as a few cents per word, while others pay a generous hourly rate, and still others, on a per-project basis.

Just like other independent business people, freelance writers must spend a good portion of their time marketing their services. This generally involves plenty of research, lots of good ideas, and many letters. The most successful freelancers take a very businesslike approach to their writing and are careful to market their services in a very professional manner. They don't wait for business to come to them. Instead they are constantly seeking out writing assignments from a variety of interesting sources.

It is quite common for freelance writers to start out writing part time in addition to holding down another job. They continue to moonlight as writers until they've built up the experience and clientele to maintain a steady income from their writing.

More than anything else, it's a freelance writer's way with words that keeps the writing assignments coming. Writing well is the only credential that counts; however, education and experience can be the keys to opportunities for freelance writers to prove their skills. Most people who succeed as freelancers have a college background in fields such as liberal arts, communications, or journalism, and have gained experience working as a journalist, public relations writer, or editor. Writers with an entrepreneurial sense of adventure and deep reserves of creative ideas may find their future in freelance writing.

YOUR LIFE SO FAR

Writers are often encouraged to write what they know. One thing you know more about than anyone else (expect maybe your parents) is your life. So gather a nice notebook and something to write with and start getting your life's story down on paper. Start with an outline first—listing key events and major characters. It's up to you whether you want to do it as a straightforward nonfiction story (no lies, please!) or embellish it as a fiction story. Just be sure to indicate whichever path you choose. Once you get started, your life story may inspire other ideas—maybe a wild adventure story or a juicy mystery. Just get writing and see where your words take you.

WORDS FOR SALE

Freelance writers have to know where to find clients and how to please them. Two tools make it easier to accomplish this. Go to the reference section of your local library and find *Children's Writers and Illustrators* by Alice Pope (Cincinnati: Writers Digest, 2006) and *Literary Marketplace* (Medford, N.J.: Information Today, 2006). With these two rather bulky books, you'll have located thousands of potential clients. Take some time to thumb through and learn a little bit about some of them.

 ON THE WEB

WRITING IN CYBERSPACE

- Children's Writing Resource at http://www.write4kids.com
- Creative Writing for Kids at http://www.creativewriting4kids.com
- Headliners at http://www.headliners.org
- Kids on the Net at http://www.kidsonthenet.org.uk
- Resources for Young Writers at http://www.debbieohi.com/young

JUMPSTART YOUR WRITING CAREER

You don't have to wait until you grow up to become a writer. Web sites like those listed below provide opportunities for budding young writers to publish their work. What are you waiting for?

- Amazing Kids E-Zine at http://www.amazing-kids.org/ezine_11/ez.html
- Merlyn's Pen at http://www.merlynspen.org
- Stone Soup at http://www.stonesoup.com
- Write 4 Fun at http://www.write4fun.net
- Zuzu magazine at http://zuzu.org

AT THE LIBRARY

READ TO WRITE

Okay, all you aspiring writers out there. Sharpen your pencils and have at it with tips found in books such as:

Farrell, Tish. *Write Your Own Fantasy Story.* Mankato, Minn.: Capstone, 2006.

———. *Write Your Own Historical Fiction Story.* Mankato, Minn.: Capstone, 2006.

———. *Write Your Own Mystery Story.* Mankato, Minn.: Capstone, 2006.

———. *Write Your Own Realistic Fiction Story.* Mankato, Minn.: Capstone, 2006.

———. *Write Your Own Science Fiction Story.* Mankato, Minn.: Capstone, 2006.

Hambleton, Vicki, Cathleen Greenwood, and Mattie J. T. Stepanek. *So You Wanna be a Writer?* Hillsboro, Ore.: Beyond Words, 2001.

Levine, Gail Carson. *Writing Magic: Creating Stories That Fly.* New York: HarperCollins, 2006.

Olien, Rebecca. *Kids Write!: Fantasy & Sci Fi, Autobiography, Adventure & More.* Nashville, Tenn.: Ideals Press, 2006.

Rhatigan, Joe. *In Print!: 40 Cool Publishing Projects for Kids.* Asheville, N.C.: Lark Books, 2004.

WITH THE EXPERTS

American Medical Writers Association
40 West Gude Drive, Suite 101
Rockville, MD 20850-1192
http://www.amwa.org

American Society of Journalists and Authors
1501 Broadway, Suite 302
New York, NY 10036-5505
http://www.asja.org

National Education Writers Association
2122 P Street NW, Suite 201
Washington, DC 20037-1037
http://www.ewa.org

National Writers Association
10940 South Parker Road, Suite 508
Parker, CO 80134-7440
http://www.nationalwriters.com

Writers-Editors Network
PO Box A
North Stratford, NH 03590-0167
http://www.writers-editors.com

GET ACQUAINTED

Naomi Wax, Freelance Writer

CAREER PATH

CHILDHOOD ASPIRATION: To be a poet or writer.

FIRST JOB: Playground duty for a parks and recreation program.

CURRENT JOB: Freelance writer and editor.

BEATING THE SYSTEM

Naomi Wax is unusual in that she has been a freelance writer and editor from day one of her professional career. She says that probably 99 percent of freelance writers start out working in-house for a magazine or book publisher, get some experience, make some contacts, and then go out on their own. Of course, she didn't know that at the time. Sometimes ignorance is bliss!

Wax graduated from the University of Michigan with a degree in English. The first two years out of school were spent traveling around Egypt, Jordan, and Turkey. She returned to live in New York City and got a job working as a waitress until she could figure out what she really wanted to do with her life. She knew she wanted to work in publishing, but she also knew that she didn't want to start at the bottom and spend a couple years typing and filing as an editorial assistant. She had nothing to lose, so she put together a résumé and sent letters offering editing and proofreading services to several book packagers. This wasn't the standard approach for breaking into the publishing industry, but it worked.

A LUCKY BREAK

Wax says the turning point for her career came when she met the head of the research department at *Condé Nast Traveler*, a travel magazine. It just so happened that the magazine was getting ready to publish several articles on Israel and needed someone who knew something about the country to verify some details. Since Wax had just spent a year there, she was hired as a fact-checker.

This project got her foot in the door and helped her make contacts that launched her career as a freelance writer and editor. Wax now realizes that it was a smart move to start out in the research department. Research work allowed her to work closely with the articles and with a variety of editors. She learned a lot about so many different things and made great contacts with people who continue to be sources of work and encouragement.

ALL IN A DAY'S WORK

Wax loves the freedom and the variety that come with being a freelance writer. Being self-employed, she is free to choose her own hours and the types of projects she works on. Since she loves to travel, it is not unusual for her to work day and night for a few months and then take off for a few weeks to some intriguing part of the world such as Turkey, Ecuador, or Peru.

Working on a wide variety of projects keeps things fun. For instance, recent assignments have included writing biographical sketches about women writers, an in-depth magazine article about estate tax law, and a short piece on her experience in Turkey for a travel magazine. Another project was doing a major overhaul on an Internet Web site for a travel magazine.

Depending on the project, Wax may work from home or on-site at a client's office. A project may last for a few days or for a few months. She accepts a variety of projects that involve writing, editing, research, training, or a combination of these skills. She's found that having the option to mix and match her skills helps prevent burnout and keeps her ready to tackle the next challenge—whatever that may be!

A LITTLE OF THIS, A LITTLE OF THAT

Wax does quite a bit of work for magazines and has, researched or had articles published in magazines such as *Condé Nast Traveler*, *Vanity Fair*, *Mirabella*, and *Elle*. Her articles tend to focus on book reviews, current events/culture, science/medicine/health, travel, and business. In fact, Wax is working on perfecting the art of the working vacation. Whenever she has the itch to go somewhere, she pitches story ideas. That way every vacation is an almost all-expenses-paid vacation (there are still a few kinks in the plan)!

Wax has also written articles for various books. Two examples are *Cool Women: The Reference* (Los Angeles: Girl Press, 1998) and the *Encyclopedia of New York City* (New Haven, Conn: Yale University Press, 1995). Look for these books in the library and see what can happen when someone with a lot of talent and initiative creates a job for him or herself.

Grant Writer

SKILL SET

- ✔ BUSINESS
- ✔ TALKING
- ✔ WRITING

SHORTCUTS

GO do some extra chores and donate your earnings to a nonprofit organization whose work you admire.

READ about some prominent nonprofit organizations such as the American Red Cross, the American Humane Society, or the Public Broadcasting System.

TRY writing a proposal to your parent(s) asking for a raise in your allowance.

WHAT IS A GRANT WRITER?

Grant writers are expert at asking for money. They approach carefully selected corporations, foundations, the government, and wealthy individuals to request money for nonprofit organizations or charities. The catch is that the giver gets nothing in return except the knowledge that he or she has used money to do something good (and get a few tax breaks); therefore, soliciting grant money works best when the grant writer asks someone to support programs that fit with the interests of that individual. For instance, a grant writer for a university might ask a former graduate (who also happens to be a multimillionaire) to help fund a new science facility. This simple strategy changes the dynamics of the process from begging for money to matching money with opportunities to make a difference.

Grant writers must use words to paint compelling pictures of the projects that need funding. Since they are generally dealing with busy people who have little time to wade through well-intentioned junk mail, they must be able to describe complex projects in concise, well-defined terms. Quite simply, they must make it as easy as possible for a donor to say yes and write a check.

Although writing is a big part of the job, it's only one part of it. Before a grant writer sits down to write a proposal, he or she has to do lots of homework. A grant writer must know just about everything about the nonprofit organization represented in the proposal. An extra dose of persuasive passion is added to the process when the writer really believes in the work being done by the organization.

Another of a grant writer's homework assignments is finding out as much as possible about the people and organizations being asked for money. Fortunately, many groups with an interest in charitable giving publish reports and other documents that provide helpful background information. Grant writers look for additional information at the library and in the newspaper to understand fully the organization's interests and giving patterns.

Quite often grant writers find that it is not enough to just know about someone or some organization. It also helps to get personally acquainted with the people behind the checkbooks. Networking and building relationships with funders is often part of a grant writer's job.

Grant writers are generally employed in the development department of nonprofit organizations. In a small organization, a grant writer may be the entire development department. In larger companies, a development director, or development officer, may head a whole team. And, instead of actually employing grant writers, some organizations may hire freelance writers to prepare grant proposals.

As with many writing careers, there isn't a direct path into grant writing. Some grant writers have experience in other kinds of writing, while others have a background in public affairs or nonprofit administration. Quite often, grant writers land in their positions by discovering a perfect fit for their writing skills in helping further a cause that is important to them.

Although there isn't a particular college degree associated with grant writing, many grant writers find it well worth the time and effort to take courses in grant writing. These courses are offered by various colleges and professional associations and can help you learn the ropes of this very specialized type of writing. Grant writing can be a good choice for a writer who likes people and wants to use his or her talent to make the world a better place. There's nothing quite like a writer with a cause.

TRY IT OUT

JOIN THE CLUB

Nonprofit organizations everywhere would welcome your interest in volunteering. Even though you don't get paid, carefully chosen volunteer projects will give you two important benefits. First, you get a chance to lend a hand to a cause you believe in or enjoy. Second, it gives you experience and contacts for future reference.

Be prepared: Most volunteering involves varying degrees of behind-the-scenes drudge work. Play it smart, and give every task your best effort. These things have a way of paying big dividends down the road.

HELPFUL WORDS

Sometimes it's hard to believe but there are a lot of children who go to bed hungry every night, even here in America. Good thing that you're a kid because kids can make a difference. One way you can help is to use words to let people know about the problem and to provide some ideas for solutions. So sit down and write a letter to your local newspaper, your local Congressman, or even the president of the United States to let them know what you think about the problem.

To find out what other kids are doing to solve some of the world's problems, go online to Web sites such as:

- Just Give at http://www.justgive.org/html/kidscorner/inspiringkids.html
- Kids Can Make a Difference at http://www.kidscanmakeadifference.org
- Kids Helping Kids at http://www.kidshelping.org

LEND A HAND

If your school is like most schools, you'll find plenty of opportunities to ask people for money. Whether it's selling candy bars for the sports team or finding advertising sponsors for the yearbook, there are plenty of ways to start learning how to ask for money.

The next time your school has a fund-raiser, get involved. Do all you can to make it a success. While you are at it, keep your eyes and ears open, and notice what kinds of projects work the best. Talk to people who sell the most, and find out the secrets to their success. It might even be useful to put together a little report to share your findings with the teachers or coaches in charge of the project.

ON THE WEB

ONLINE HELPERS

The Internet is where you can find out about all your favorite funders. Pick any major corporation, use a Web browser to find their Web site, and find out how (and if) they give back to their communities.

While you're online, take a look at some of these useful sites.

- Habitat for Humanity at http://www.habitat.org
- Humane Society at http://www.hsus.org
- International Red Cross at http://www.redcross.org
- Salvation Army at http://www.salvationarmy.org
- Save the Children at http://savethechildren.org
- Sierra Club at http://www.sierraclub.org

 AT THE LIBRARY

CHARITABLE CASE STUDIES

Find out more about some of the world's most important philanthropic organizations in the following books:

Grant, R.G. *Amnesty International.* New York: Chelsea House, 2006.

Hastings, Terry. *The Peace Corps.* New York: Chelsea House, 2006.

Parry, Ann. *Doctors Without Borders.* New York: Chelsea House, 2006.

———. *Red Cross.* New York: Chelsea House, 2006.

———. *Save the Children.* New York: Chelsea House, 2006.

WITH THE EXPERTS

Alliance for Nonprofit Management
1899 L Street NW, 6th Floor
Washington, DC 20036-3804
http://www.allianceonline.org

Association of Fundraising Professionals
4300 Wilson Boulevard, Suite 300
Arlington, VA 22203-4179
http://www.afpnet.org

Foundation Center
79 Fifth Avenue, 16th Floor
New York, NY 10003-3076
http://foundationcenter.org

Independent Sector
1200 18th Street NW, Suite 200
Washington, DC 20036-2529
http://www.independentsector.org

GET ACQUAINTED

Elizabeth Curtler, Grant Writer

CAREER PATH

CHILDHOOD ASPIRATION: To work for the State Department in other countries or to be a newspaper reporter.

FIRST JOB: A summer secretary for the U.S. Department of Education.

CURRENT JOB: Assistant vice president of foundation, corporate, and government relations at the University of Richmond.

FIRST IMPRESSIONS ARE LASTING IMPRESSIONS

Elizabeth Curtler believes that a person's first work experience can play an important part in establishing the direction that his or her career takes. For instance, one summer when she was in college, she worked for a government agency that was responsible for awarding fellowships to students pursuing higher learning experiences. This work experience, along with her jobs as an English teacher and a community college administrator, gave her a place to put her words to work. She's been writing to help various academic institutions raise funds for a number of years now.

EVERY DAY IS A LEARNING EXPERIENCE

Working as Curtler does in a university provides a fascinating opportunity to learn about a wide variety of subjects. Curtler has been involved in writing proposals for projects that involve subjects as diverse as automobile safety, chemistry animation, Korean studies, and contemporary art. Although there are times that she claims to know about as much about a given subject as you could hold in a very small thimble, she takes every opportunity to ask questions about what each project involves and why it is important.

Curtler is in charge of the Office of Foundation, Corporate and Government Relations at the University of Richmond. Her office helps the faculty, staff, and administration at the university find and manage grants (money!) from a wide variety of public and private sources. These grants provide the funds necessary to support special research projects and creative work. It's a big job! You can find out more about what Curtler does at her office's Web site at http://oncampus.richmond.edu/academics/grants.

EVERY WORD COUNTS

When Curtler approaches a foundation or corporation, she is often asking for millions of dollars to fund very important work. With that much at stake, it's worth taking the time to learn as much as she can about each project. It's also extremely important that Curtler use good judgment in matching the right funders with the right projects. That takes lots of homework, but it pays off when those big checks show up in the mailbox.

A LAST RESORT

Curtler says that writing is hard work. So hard, in fact, that she doesn't sit down at her computer to write a grant proposal until she's sure the time is right. Two things tell her it's time to get writing. First, everyone involved in the project knows what to say. That means that the ideas about the proposed project have been hammered out enough so that its purpose is clear and easily defined. Second, the people Curtler's approaching for funds are ready to hear what the proposal has to say. Reaching this stage of the process involves using two types of skills—verbal communication skills and people skills. Curtler must invest time and energy in developing relationships with people before asking them for money. It's one of her favorite parts of the job.

THANK GOODNESS FOR DEADLINES

Even after writing professionally for a number of years, Curtler sometimes finds herself at a loss for words. She says it can be a challenge to get started on a new project. Fortunately, she works under a lot of deadlines, so sometimes she has no choice but to sit down and just write. Curtler calls this being backed in a corner by a deadline.

One thing that helps her get going is knowing that the first thing she writes is never final. There's always the opportunity to go back and make it better.

A FEW WORDS FOR FUTURE WRITERS

The more you read, the better you write, says Curtler. She urges those with an itch to write to read all kinds of new things. Everything you read gives you new ideas about words and the way they are used.

As for learning to become a writer, Curtler believes that doing it—writing—is the only way to learn it. One way to get practice is to share your writing talent with people and organizations who might need it—your church or synagogue, a volunteer organization, or even a family member. Writing is something you can do to help others.

Information Professional

SKILL SET

- ✔ ADVENTURE
- ✔ COMPUTERS
- ✔ WRITING

SHORTCUTS

GO to the library and browse through the books in the reference section.

READ *Scholastic Book of Lists* by James Buckley, Jr. (New York: Scholastic, 2006).

TRY picking a subject of interest and seeing how much information you can dig up about it.

WHAT IS AN INFORMATION PROFESSIONAL?

Information professionals, sometimes called *information brokers*, are part researcher, part writer, and part investigator. Often hired to find the most obscure and elusive types of information, information professionals must exhaust every resource on the trail of the answer. Chasing down elusive information often sends information professionals cruising down the information highway.

In fact, computers and other technology were the catalysts that started this whole profession in the first place. The Internet, CD-ROM databases, and other sources of information opened a whole world of resources for skilled information professionals to glean from. These resources put at one's fingertips information that might otherwise take days or weeks of painstaking research (and sometimes extensive travel) to find.

The information is out there. However, as anyone who has tried to find specific information on the Internet can attest, it takes skill and resourcefulness to navigate the system in search of what you need. In addition to all the high-tech methods, an information professional is also no stranger to libraries, news files, government record agencies, and other sources of hard-to-find information.

Information professionals are sometimes employed by corporations but are just as likely to be self-employed. Self-employed information professionals can work from a home office or from a business suite. Clients from anywhere in the world can be served efficiently thanks to the convenience and affordability of technology such as computers, faxes, and modems, and the efficiency of overnight mail. Who needs to know that the information professional is sitting at the kitchen table working in pajamas?

An information professional may serve a variety of different types of clients—anything from a start-up business to a major Fortune 500 conglomerate. Some specialize in a particular area such as medical research, legal issues, or other technical research. Advertising agencies and public relations firms are frequent users of information professionals, as are publishing houses and educational institutions.

A profession closely related to that of information professional is that of researcher. Publishers of magazines, reference books, and other types of nonfiction books often have a research staff who use their skills in two ways. One way is to verify the facts found in complex articles or soon-to-be published books. The other way is to collect new information for projects that are in

progress. The latter is called primary research and is usually the domain of more experienced researchers.

Working on the research side of publishing can be a great way to learn about a particular subject or about publishing in general. Since researchers often have to rewrite incorrect data or compile reports detailing their findings, it also provides an opportunity to gain valuable writing skills.

As for training requirements, there are none officially. If you've got the equipment, the skills, and the clients, you are in business. There's a catch, of course. The skills and the clients are likely to be more readily available with training and experience on your résumé. Some of the most successful information professionals and researchers have a background in library science, which allowed them to master some of the finer arts of in-depth research.

THE INFORMATION PROFESSIONAL TEST, PART 1

You think you'd like to be an information professional or researcher, do you? Take this little test to see if you've got the right stuff.

Go to the reference section of a well-stocked library and see how long it takes to find the answers to the following questions.

- In what year did Grover Cleveland begin his second term as president of the United States and what was unusual about it?
- What was the birthplace of author Mark Twain (aka Samuel Clemens)?
- What was the batting average of baseball great Babe Ruth?

By the way, feel free to ask for help if you need it. Any good information professional knows when it's time to call in reinforcements.

THE INFORMATION PROFESSIONAL TEST, PART 2

Back for more, are you? This time park yourself in front of a computer with an Internet connection. Go back to the same three questions and use your favorite Internet search engine such as Google (http://www.google.com) or Yahoo (http://www.yahoo.com) to find the answers.

Make a chart to compare the results of the library versus Internet research. Which method was quickest? Which provided the most accurate information? What method was easiest to use to find the information you needed?

SHAKE THE FAMILY TREE

Tracing your family's history can provide an interesting and informative introduction to the research process. Start by asking questions. Ask parents, grandparents, and other relatives for details about other branches of the family tree. Record everything you discover and how you discovered it.

Then go online and use a free map resource such as Multimap (http://www.multimap.com) to print out a world map. Use a marker to trace what you learned about where your family came from and where they settled. If your family is currently spread out over the United States or elsewhere, print out another map and put big dots on all the places where family members now live.

CHECK IT OUT

ON THE WEB

CRUISING FOR ANSWERS

For the first time in history people (like you!) now have access to a world of information via the Internet. And it's all just a click of a mouse away. See what new and interesting things you can learn at kid-friendly research Web sites such as:

- AOL@School at http://www.aolatschool.com/students
- Ask for Kids at http://www.askforkids.com
- Cybersleuth Kids at http://cybersleuth-kids.com

- Kids Click! at http://www.kidsclick.org
- Yahooligans.com at http://kids.yahoo.com

AT THE LIBRARY

TOOLS OF THE TRADE

Libraries, as you might suspect, are one of an information professional's favorite hangouts. You'll understand why when you see how much information you can find in books such as:

Masoff, Joy. *Oh Yikes! History's Grossest Moments.* New York: Workman, 2006.

Miller, Millie. *Our World: A Country-by-Country Guide.* New York: Scholastic, 2006.

Roberts, David, and Jeremy Leslie. *Pick Me Up.* New York: DK Publishing, 2006.

Weber, Belinda. *The Kingfisher Children's Atlas.* New York: Houghton Mifflin, 2004.

World Almanac. *World Almanac for Kids 2007.* New York: World Almanac, 2006.

———. *Yo! I Know: Brain-Building Quizzes.* New York: World Almanac, 2006.

Also, you can find all kinds of great information about topics ranging from ancient Greece to baseball and castles to spies in an illustrated series of books called *DK Eyewitness* (New York: DK Publishing). With a couple hundred titles in the series, there's something for everyone. Ask a teacher or librarian to help you find a title that suits your fancy.

WITH THE EXPERTS

American Society for Information Science and Technology
1320 Fenwick Lane, Suite 510
Silver Spring, MD 20910-3560
http://www.asis.org

Association of Independent Information Professionals
8550 United Plaza Boulevard, Suite 1001
Baton Rogue, LA 70809-0200
http://www.aiip.org

GET ACQUAINTED

Mary Ellen Bates,
Information Professional

CAREER PATH

CHILDHOOD ASPIRATION: To be a sign-language interpreter, or a doctor, or a librarian.

FIRST JOB: Waitress at an all-night coffee shop.

CURRENT JOB: Owner of Bates Information Services, a research and consulting company.

BACKGROUND INFORMATION

Ask Mary Ellen Bates how she got into the information business and she'll tell you that she stumbled into it. Back in the late 1970s, she landed a job as a database manager for the library of a law firm. She admits that she's not at all sure why she was hired since her college degree was in mathematical philosophy and she had utterly no knowledge of computers. Once there, she discovered that she really liked working in libraries, so she continued the job while attending the University of California, Berkeley, where she earned a master's degree in library and information science.

After that she worked for over 10 years in specialized libraries—not public libraries, but libraries within the federal government, the court system, and within private companies. By 1990 she had reached two conclusions. First, she really enjoyed doing research and working with clients. Second, she liked running her own show. She had heard about people with her background and skills starting businesses as information brokers or information entrepreneurs, so she spent about a year planning and then launched her own company, Bates

Information Services, in 1991. Now she is a nationally recognized expert in the field.

TRADE SECRETS

Bates shares that she learned many valuable lessons from working in libraries that help her succeed as an information entrepreneur. For instance, she knows how to conduct research cost-effectively and efficiently, which, with clients paying an hourly rate for her services, is a much-appreciated skill. She also learned how to "manage" clients and how to conduct an effective information-needs interview. After all those years in the library, staying current on new information resources and search techniques is second nature to her and writing reports for clients is a breeze (well, at the very least she's got a lot of experience doing it).

When it comes to tackling specific projects, she tends to spend some time educating herself about the subject matter at hand. She admits that, while she's not an expert in most of her clients areas, she knows how to find the information she needs to become an expert. Here's the process for some research she used when working on a project for the golf equipment industry:

- First, she went to a couple of specialized sources that taught her some basic information about the golf equipment industry such as http://www.hoovers.com and http://www.marketresearch.com.
- Then she ran a search in two or three search engines to see what basic resources she could find. A visit to http://www.A9.com provided pointers about some of the best reference sources.
- Next she checked out the Web sites of several associations of golf equipment manufacturers to see what information they had.
- After that she scanned several news sources to see what the latest developments were in the industry and searched the U.S. Patent & Trademark Office (http://www.uspto.gov) to see who had recently patented new golf equipment.

- Last, but not least, she used several of the professional online services like http://www.Dialog.com, http://www.Factiva.com, and http://www.LexisNexis.com to find information from trade and professional publications that are not available to the general public on the Web.

In addition to the golf equipment project, other interesting subjects Bates has explored on behalf of clients include the origins of bungee jumping, all the possible uses for a new carbide blade, and the disaster-recovery plans for every county in the country.

STUMP THE EXPERT

Every once in a while even a seasoned professional like Bates comes across a question for which there just *isn't* an answer. Questions that have stumped her include one about how many flags were sold after September 11. It was a large number but no one seems to know for sure how many. She's also discovered that it's next to impossible to find out how often a company's network is hacked. Apparently, that is inside information that companies will not share.

When this happens she looks for something close, or something that might suggest the answer. For instance, for the flag question she might contact the National Flag Foundation or the National Retail Federation or perhaps look for indications of an increase in sales of patriotic-themed greeting cards, and so on. Bates says there is always some way to find information on a project, even if it's not exactly what the client hoped to find.

FUTURE INFORMATION PROFESSIONALS BE ADVISED

Information professionals need to be creative, flexible, interested in lots of different stuff, and persistent. The best researchers are the ones with broad backgrounds in lots of different subjects. You don't have to be an expert in every subject, but curiosity and creativity will get you far!

Journalist

SKILL SET

- ✔ ADVENTURE
- ✔ TALKING
- ✔ WRITING

SHORTCUTS

GO visit the offices of a newspaper and get a sense of the fast-paced, no-nonsense side of journalism.

READ national and local newspapers and magazines to see how journalists write about the news.

TRY writing a story about an event at your school for the community newspaper.

WHAT IS A JOURNALIST?

Who won the 2006 World Series? What's going on in the Middle East? Should you wear a coat to school tomorrow? If you know the answers to these questions, chances are that it is because of the work of a journalist. Journalists, or reporters, are the people who write stories about the people, places, and events that shape our world. The latest news about sports and fashion, as well as developments in Third World countries and outer space, are brought to our doorstep and television sets compliments of journalists who meticulously track down the facts and report them in news stories.

Writing late-breaking news is quite a bit different from other kinds of writing. Articles must be factual, informative, free from the reporter's bias, and concise. Reporters must continually find new ways to build stories around the six key elements of a journalistic report: who, what, where, when, why, and how.

Successful journalists must develop a nose for news and be able to make quick decisions about whether a particular event is news or not. They often must wrestle with ethical dilemmas such as when the public's right to information overrides a person's right to privacy.

Probably the most consistent challenge facing any journalist is the time-crunch issue. Stories of even the utmost importance must be investigated and written quickly and accurately. Competition between various news sources makes this even more of a rush as everyone wants to "scoop," or be first with, a new story. Once a newspaper hits the streets, there is no way to take it back, so journalists have to get the story right the first time.

The work of a given journalist might be as routine as covering a local school board meeting or as heartbreaking as covering the aftermath of a terrible tragedy. Some journalists, particularly those reporting from war zones or in other volatile situations, work under life-threatening circumstances.

Journalists are typically assigned a "beat" and work on specific types of stories such as local news, sports, or education. No matter what beat they are assigned, effective journalists share two traits. One trait is curiosity. Journalists have to be full of questions. The second trait is persistence.

Journalists must have the energy and drive to do what it takes to find the answers.

If you'd like to become a journalist, plan on earning a college degree in journalism, communications, English, or political science. Also, plan on starting at the bottom of the ladder in the newsroom. The most exciting stories tend to go to the more experienced journalists. Make sure to take advantage of every opportunity to get experience by working on school newspapers and actively seeking internship opportunities while you complete your education.

Perhaps the best perk of the job is that thousands and even millions of people might read a journalist's work each day. This is a privilege that few other writing professions enjoy. Journalists get the opportunity to have a major impact on their world. Wars, environmental debates, and many a political career have been won or lost via the power of the press.

TRY IT OUT

FOLLOW THAT STORY!

Look in the first section of a major newspaper and find a major story. It might be about a natural disaster, a political issue, or an international event. Cut out the headline story and any associated stories, sidebars, or charts. Continue to follow the story until its resolution. Keep track of significant details and take note of how the story is reintroduced to readers on subsequent days. Make sure to note which page the story appears on each day as this will provide important clues to the story's continued importance in the scheme of world news. You'll also want to keep track of the reporters! Is it the same person every day? Does it vary?

If possible, follow the story from more than one source. Take notes about coverage on various television and radio stations. Read and clip stories about the same event that appear in other newspapers. Check the Internet or your library's microfiche files for related coverage. Compare the stories and how they are covered. Notice what elements are emphasized in each story. Can you identify the reporter's angle? Can you detect any bias in the report?

GO AFTER THE NEWS

It goes without saying that if you want to be a journalist, you should work on the school newspaper or yearbook. Both of these outlets can provide invaluable first experiences in scooping out news events, covering them, and writing stories to inform. Keep copies of your best work to include in your professional portfolio.

ON THE WEB

INSTANT NEWS

We've got fast food, so why not fast news? The Internet is the source of news as it happens, when it happens. Find out how journalists keep the world informed on the information highway by visiting some of these hot news spots:

- http://www.abcnews.go.com
- http://www.cbsnews.com
- http://www.cnn.com
- http://www.foxnews.com
- http://www.msnbc.msn.com
- National Geographic Kids News at http://news.nationalgeographic.com/kids
- Scholastic News Online at http://teacher.scholastic.com/scholasticnews/games_quizzes/index.asp

AT THE LIBRARY

READ ALL ABOUT IT!

Following are some interesting books for you to read about journalists and their work.

Ali, Dominic, and Michael Cho. *Media Madness: An Insider's Guide to Media*. Tonawanda, N.Y.: Kids Can Press, 2005.
Craig, Tom. *Media Wise: Internet Technology, People, Process*. Mankato, Minn.: Smart Apple, 2004.
Ferguson. *Careers in Focus: Journalism*. New York: Ferguson, 2005.
Gifford, Clive. *Eyewitness: Media and Communications*. New York: DK Publishing, 1999.
Jones, Sarah. *Film Technology, People, Process*. Mankato, Minn.: Smart Apple, 2003.
Petley, Julian. *Media Wise: Newspapers and Magazines*. Mankato, Minn.: Smart Apple, 2003.
Reeves, Diane Lindsey. *Virtual Apprentice: TV Journalist*. New York: Ferguson, 2007.
Sullivan, George. *Journalists at Risk: Reporting America's Wars*. Minneapolis: Lerner, 2004.

A NOSE FOR NEWS

Find yourself hot on the trail of some newsworthy adventures in these books featuring young, fictional news reporters:

Ellerbee, Linda. *Get Real #1: Girl Reporter Blows Lid Off Town*. New York: Harper Collins, 2000.
Feinsten, John. *Last Shot: A Final Four Mystery*. New York: Random House, 2006.
Givner, Joan. *Ellen Fremedon: Journalist*. Toronto, Ont.: Groundwood, 2006.
Speregen, Debra Newberger. *Miss O and Friends: Caught in the 'Net*. New York: Watson Guptill, 2006.
Trembath, Don. *The Popsicle Journal*. Custer, Wash.: Orca Books, 2002.

WITH THE EXPERTS

American Society of Journalists
and Authors
1501 Broadway, Suite 302
New York, NY 10036-5505
http://www.asja.org

American Society of
Newspaper Editors
11690-B Sunrise Valley Drive
Reston, VA 20191-1409
http://www.asne.org

Dow Newspaper Fund
4300 Route One North
South Brunswick, NJ 08852
http://djnewspaperfund
.dowjones.com

National Newspaper
Association
127-129 Neff Avenue
Columbia, MO 65211-1200
http://www.nna.org

Newspaper Guild
501 Third Street NW
Washington, DC 20001-2797
http://www.newsguild.org

Society of Professional
Journalists
Eugene S. Pulliam National
Journalism Center
3909 North Meridian Street
Indianapolis, IN 46209-4011
http://www.spj.org

GET ACQUAINTED

Debbie Becker, Journalist

CAREER PATH

CHILDHOOD ASPIRATION: To be a forest ranger.

FIRST JOB: Worked as a gofer for the *Washington Post.*

CURRENT JOB: Sports reporter for *USA Today.*

THE RIGHT PLACE AT THE RIGHT TIME

Along with a talent for writing and knowledge of a number of sports, Debbie Becker also has a knack for being in the right place at the right time. She landed a job with the *Washington Post* by joking with a friend to put in a good word for her with his editor. He did, and she got a job.

The same holds true with her present job. *USA Today* was just a new, upstart newspaper when Becker graduated from college, and they immediately hired her. Today the paper is read by some 2 million readers every weekday.

A WOMAN IN A MAN'S WORLD

As a freshman lacrosse player at the American University in Washington, D.C., Becker was disappointed to find out that the school paper covered only men's sports events. When she went to the office to complain, she found out that the only reason women's sports weren't covered was because there was no one to write the stories. Becker volunteered to start reporting on these neglected events, discovered she liked it, and a career was born.

Sports is still a male-dominated world, and Becker often finds herself as the only woman in the press box at many events. To get where she is today, Becker has had to work extra hard and watch her step, but she wouldn't trade the experience for anything.

OLYMPIC-SIZED BEAT

Becker has reported on five Olympic events including competitions in Nagano, Japan; Calgary, Canada; Barcelona, Spain; Atlanta, Georgia; and Salt Lake City. She specializes in covering gymnastic, figure skating, and cycling events. This beat involves more than just covering the main Olympic games. Long before the world gathers to compete, there are trials and national championships to keep track of. Becker particularly likes doing stories on unknown athletes in minor sports and on women athletes because it gives her a chance to recognize people who've worked hard and are often overlooked.

THIS JOB HAS PERKS

Olympics, World Series, Super Bowl—Becker has been there, done that, seen it. As a journalist, Becker gets to see lots of events for free—the same events that others pay top dollar for, if they can get tickets at all.

ADVICE TO FUTURE SPORTS JOURNALISTS

Get all the internship experience you can so that you can find out what you like and what you're good at. Becker had originally planned to get into television broadcasting, but an internship experience taught her that she didn't like it at all, so she refocused her attention on newspapers.

Librarian

SKILL SET

- ✔ COMPUTERS
- ✔ WRITING
- ✔ TALKING

SHORTCUTS

GO visit every library you can find—school, public, corporate, law, etc.

READ *Booklist Online*, a journal from the American Library Association, at http://www.booklistonline.com. Be sure to review the latest news about books for youth.

TRY creating a mini-library with your own book collection.

WHAT IS A LIBRARIAN?

Keeping rowdy readers in line is just one small part of a librarian's job. According to the American Library Association, librarians are professionals who organize and preserve recordable information and knowledge, provide library and information services, and deliver information products.

On first guess, you might think of a librarian (sometimes called a *multimedia specialist*) as the person who helps you find information for research papers and check out books. If so, you are only partially correct. This type of librarian works in an area called *user services*, which involves dealing directly with the public (the users of a library). Places where you might find this type of librarian at work include the reference section of the library, the circulation desk, and the children's department.

Another type of library work is *technical services*. These librarians work behind the scenes acquiring new books and materials, cataloging books for the library's database, and otherwise preparing and protecting the materials that are placed on the library shelves.

The third area of library work is in *administration*. Much like any other business or government agency, someone must handle the day-to-day operations that keep a library running smoothly. Administrative duties may include managing the people who work in a library, ordering equipment and supplies, planning and keeping track of budgets and expenses, raising funds to support the library, and handling public relations. It is an especially good choice for someone who has an interest in the business side of the library.

In addition to these three main types of library work, there are increasing opportunities for blending expertise in computer technology with a library career. In the past, most libraries kept track of their collections with card catalogs. New computer automated information retrieval systems make the process much easier and efficient. Professionals with the skills needed to plan and operate these highly specialized computer systems are in big demand.

Librarians of all types can be found in several different kinds of libraries. You may already be familiar with the public library and your school library or multimedia center. Other places where librarians work are in academic libraries at colleges and universities and special libraries that serve organizations such as businesses, government agencies, museums, law firms, and medical centers. Special libraries offer librarians an opportunity to blend a personal interest such as art or medicine with their general interest in books.

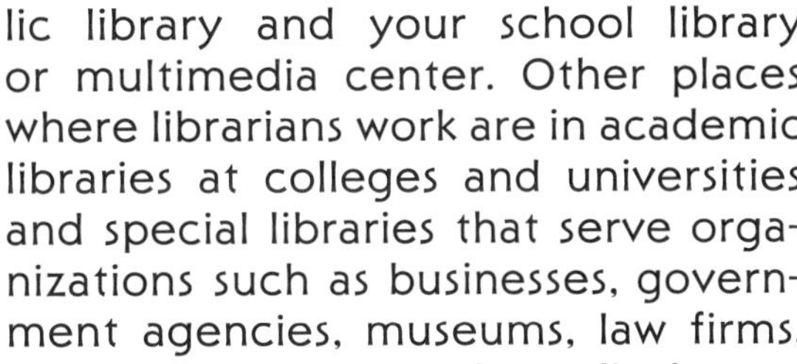

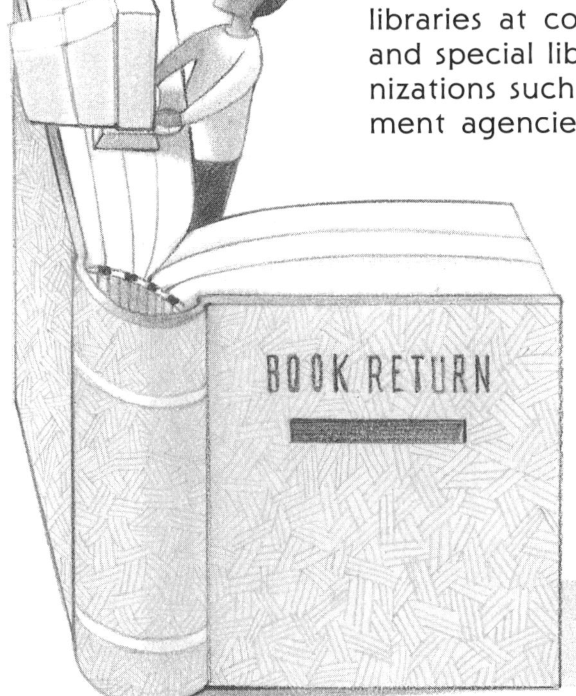

To become a full-fledged librarian, you'll need a

master's degree in library science from a program accredited by the American Library Association. You can earn your undergraduate degree in almost any area, although some would say that a well-rounded liberal arts education might be an ideal choice. In the meantime, while you are earning your degrees, there are many opportunities to work in a library as an assistant or technician.

New technology and the information highway continue to pave the way for exciting new opportunities for librarians as information managers. If working with books, people, information, and technology sounds like a winning combination for your future, read on.

TRY IT OUT

TEACH SOMEONE TO READ

It seems fairly logical that if you are interested in libraries, you're probably a pretty big fan of books as well. If that's true for you, you've already discovered what a great treasure it is to be able to read.

There are many people, however, of your own age as well as older and younger people, who do not know how to read. Fortunately, you can help.

One of the best ways to help a child learn to read is to read to them. Ask your teacher or school media specialist if there are any programs for older students like you to read to younger students. Make a list of the books you most enjoyed when you were little and start with those.

LEND SOME TIME TO A LIBRARY

The best place to find out if library work is a good career choice for you is at a library. Talk to your school or public librarian about your interest, and volunteer to help out. You'll probably start out by reshelving books. Okay, so it can get a bit tedious, but it's a great way to learn the Dewey decimal system. Once you get going, look for other ways to help out. The children's summer reading program may be a good place to experience more of what it's like to work in a library.

Other places where you might put your newly found library skills to good use are at a church or synagogue, a health care facility for the elderly, child care centers, and neighborhood associations. Volunteering can be a fun way to prepare for your future while making life a bit brighter for others.

ON THE WEB

JUST THE FACTS, PLEASE

Books aren't the only things you find at libraries these days. For many people, the library provides their first and sometimes only access to the Internet. That's why librarians have to stay one step ahead of the rest of the crowd on the information highway. One way that they do this is by using a number of Internet resources, including:

- Children's Literature Web Guide at http://www.acs.ucalgary.ca/~dkbrown
- KidsConnect with the American Association of School Librarians at http://www.ala.org/ICONN/kctools.html
- Kids' Search Tools at http://www.rcls.org/ksearch.htm
- Librarians Internet Index at http://lii.org
- Library of Congress for Kids at http://www.loc.gov/families
- On-Lion for Kids with the New York Public Library at http://kids.nypl.org

JOIN THE CLUB

Like books? Have friends who like books? How about getting everyone together for a monthly book club? A teacher or school media specialist might be willing to sponsor an after school club or maybe your parent(s) will let you host a club at your house. The following resources will give you ideas on what to read and how to get started:

- Book Nuts Reading Club at http://www.booknutsreadingclub.com
- Kids' Reads at http://www.kidsreads.com/clubs/index.asp
- Planet Book Club at http://www.planetbookclub.com/kids
- Spaghetti Book Club at http://www.spaghettibookclub.org

Make sure to keep a log of all the books your club reads. Make notes about what everyone liked best and least about each book.

AT THE LIBRARY

LIBRARY BOOKS

Read about a famous librarian, some famous readers, and what it's like to work in a library in books such as:

Burby, Liza N. *Day in the Life of a Librarian.* New York: Rosen, 2001.

Ferguson. *Careers in Focus: Library and Information Science.* New York: Ferguson, 2006.

Forbes, Dina. E. *Laura Bush: Teacher, Librarian and First Lady.* New York: Ferguson, 2005.

Sweeney, Alyse. *Welcome to the Library.* New York: Scholastic, 2006.

Pearson, Debora, and Michele Landsberg. *When I Went to the Library: Writers Celebrate Books and Reading.* Toronto, Ont.: Groundwood, 2002.

For a little fun, try these fictional library adventure stories:

Clifford, Eth. *Help! I'm a Prisoner in the Library.* New York: Houghton Mifflin, 2004.

Peck, Richard. *Here Lies the Librarian.* New York: Penguin, 2006.

For a glimpse at how important books are to people, read:

Zusak, Markus. *The Book Thief.* New York: Random House, 2006.

WITH THE EXPERTS

American Association of Law Libraries
53 West Jackson Boulevard, Suite 940
Chicago, IL 60604-3847
http://www.aallnet.org

American Library Association
50 East Huron Street
Chicago, IL 60611-2788
http://www.ala.org

Arts Libraries Society of North America
232-239 March Road, Box 11
Ottawa, Ontario K2K 2E1
http://arlisna.org

Association of Research Libraries
21 Dupont Circle NW, Suite 800
Washington, DC 20036-1543
http://www.arl.org

Medical Library Association
65 East Wacker Place, Suite 1900
Chicago, IL 60601-7246
http://www.mlanet.org

Society of American Archivists
527 South Wells Street, 5th Floor
Chicago, IL 60607-3922
http://www.archivists.org

Special Libraries Association
331 South Patrick Street
Alexandria, VA 22314-3501
http://www.sla.org

GET ACQUAINTED

Wayne Crocker, Library Director

CAREER PATH

CHILDHOOD ASPIRATION: To be a football player.

FIRST JOB: Delivering newspapers and mowing lawns.

CURRENT JOB: Director of the Petersburg Public Library System in Virginia.

PLAN B

Like a lot of young boys, Wayne Crocker had high hopes of a career as a professional football player. All the way through school he'd played football, baseball, and basketball, and he was pretty good. When he got to high school and it came time to try out for varsity basketball, he was competing against the likes of classmate Moses Malone for a spot on the team. When Crocker didn't make the team, he realized that there might be a little more to school than playing sports. He was surprised to discover how much there was to learn and applied himself to learning all he could.

Looking back now as a grown-up, he can say that not making the team was a good thing. It helped him focus his efforts in other areas and start thinking about what to do with his life.

THE START OF A BRAND-NEW LIFE

Crocker had always been a hard worker. He started delivering newspapers when he was just 11 years old and kept busy cutting lawns for several years (he even took care of the grass at a local cemetery). One of his friends worked at the Petersburg (Virginia) Public Library and told him that they had an opening for another library page. He had not used the library very much up to that point, but working in a cool, quiet place sounded like a nice change of pace from cutting grass in the hot sun, so he applied for the job and got it. Little did he know that this opportunity would shape his entire life.

ONE GOOD TURN AFTER ANOTHER

Crocker continued working at the library all the way through college. Along the way he'd been promoted to library aide and continued to enjoy the work. During his senior year in college, the library director took him aside and encouraged him to apply for a scholarship to receive a master's degree in library science.

As a business major, Crocker had been entertaining thoughts of working for a Fortune 500 company after he graduated. But the library director was not someone who took no for an answer, so Crocker went ahead and applied for the scholarship. That's how he won a full scholarship to earn a master's in library science degree from Atlanta University.

BACK TO WHERE IT ALL BEGAN

While working on his master's degree, Crocker got a job at the Atlanta Public Library. There he worked on a retrospective conversion process in which all the books and materials in the library system were converted to a machine-readable format. It was a big job, but he worked hard and found that it all paid off when he was offered a job as a librarian in the system. Atlanta was just finishing a new state-of-the-art library, so it was a really exciting place to work.

Crocker was happily minding his own business in the job, when the same Petersburg library director who'd convinced him to apply for a scholarship decided to retire. She encouraged Crocker to apply for her job. A little reluctant at first, Crocker put in an application. The former library page got the job and went back home as director of three libraries (the main library and two branches). It was a dream come true.

HOME, SWEET HOME

The fact that Petersburg is home to Crocker makes it especially satisfying to be in such an influential position. It motivates him to get involved and make a difference in the community. His community involvement takes many forms. He's active as a mentor to young people, and he participates in a number of community boards and commissions.

IF LIBRARIES ARE IN YOUR FUTURE

Libraries aren't just four walls and books anymore. Crocker is excited about the way that computers and other technologies are turning libraries into information and communication centers. Pretty soon the library will be the place to go for contact with an entire world of information. Crocker sees an exciting future for young people who know how to learn, think, and focus. He suggests that you visit one of his favorite Web sites at http://www.librarycareers.org to find out more about having a career like his.

Literary Agent

SKILL SET

- ✔ BUSINESS
- ✔ TALKING
- ✔ WRITING

SHORTCUTS

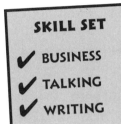

GO scrutinize several books in the children's section of the library. Choose which books you'd have been most proud to represent as a literary agent.

READ *Publishers Weekly* at http://www.publishersweekly.com. Make sure to take a peek at the children's book section.

TRY practicing your negotiating skills the next time your friends have a disagreement.

WHAT IS A LITERARY AGENT?

Literary agents are one of the links between writers and publishers. They represent authors in getting manuscripts and book proposals to editors who can publish them. To accomplish this, literary agents must wear several hats. First, they must be book critics. Out of all the manuscripts that cross their desks, literary agents must be able to pick the winners. This requires a broad yet discerning interest in books of all kinds and an understanding of what publishers look for in books. Literary agents cannot skimp on this step if they expect to be in business for long. Publishers need to be able to trust the literary judgment of the agents they work with. They count on agents to weed out the junk and send books with the potential to make it big. A literary agent must be very careful to guard his or her reputation as a reliable source of good books.

Second, literary agents must be editors. In fact many successful literary agents actually get their start in the business as editors. Wearing the editorial hat, literary agents must be able to recognize the raw potential of a manuscript, spotting those "diamonds in the rough" and guiding a writer through the process of polishing it up. Recognizing that the book may only get one shot at being picked up by a publisher, the agent wants to get the manuscript in good shape.

The third hat that literary agents wear is that of matchmaker. Literary agents have to match the right book with the right publisher. They have to know the special interests of each publisher and make connections with key decision-makers in the business. Literary agents who know how to "work the crowd" and meet editors and publishers at conventions, trade shows, and other publishing events have an edge over those who simply submit manuscripts with a polite cover letter attached.

Business manager is another hat worn by literary agents. Once an agent carefully selects a promising project, fine-tunes the manuscript, and finds a good publisher, it is time to close the sale. Authors depend on their agents to negotiate the best possible terms for their work. This part of the process can get rather complicated when issues such as royalties, copyright, foreign rights, and (for the ever-hopeful fiction writers) movie rights enter the picture. Some literary agents have a legal background or seek legal counsel for this part of the process.

Since literary agents work on commission and get paid only when a book is sold, they are very picky about the authors they choose to represent. In addition to representing writers, some agents work with songwriters and playwrights as well. Literary agents may work in an established agency or start their own.

Most literary agents find that training and experience in the publishing industry is essential to their success. A college background in journalism, English, communications, marketing, or even law can provide effective training for this profession.

TRY IT OUT

READ 'EM AND WEEP

Most major newspapers include literary reviews in their Sunday editions. Here book critics express their sometimes brutally honest opinions about books of various genres (categories such as mystery, self-help, etc.). Read through the review section of your local newspaper or go online to read what the critics at the *New York Times* have to say at http// www.nytimes.com.

Go online to read what the critics at the *New York Times* have to say about the latest children's titles at http://www.nytimes.com/pages/books/bestseller/index.html (and click on "children's books).

Make a chart with two columns. Put a happy face at the top of one column and a sad face at the top of the other. Read each review as if you were the literary agent who sold the book or the author who wrote it. If the review says mostly good things about the book, write its title in the happy face column. If the review says mostly bad things about the book, write its title in the sad face column.

CHECK IT OUT

ON THE WEB

THE INSIDE TRACK

The Internet provides some exciting resources for you to investigate the results of a literary agent's work. Visit the Web sites of these popular children's book publishers to find out who publishes your favorite authors:

- Dorling Kindersley (DK) at http://www.kiddk.com
- Harper Collins at http://www.harpercollinschildrens.com/HarperChildrens/Kids
- Random House at http://www.randomhouse.com/kids
- Scholastic at http://scholastic.com/kids
- Simon & Schuster at http://www.simonsayskids.com

 AT THE LIBRARY

THE INSIDE STORY

Literary agents have to know what it takes to pick a winner and push it to the top of the book business. You can get a jumpstart on the process by learning all you can about the publishing world in books such as:

Camenson, Blythe. *Careers in Publishing*. New York: McGraw-Hill, 2002.

Eberts, Marjorie, and Margaret Gisler. *Careers for Bookworms and Other Literary Types*. New York: McGraw-Hill, 2002.

Yager, Fred, and Jan Yager. *Career Opportunities in the Publishing Industry*. New York: Ferguson, 2005.

MEET MY AUTHOR

As you read about some of the following famous authors, imagine what it would be like to represent someone like them someday.

Marcovitz, Hal. *Who Wrote That? Maurice Sendak*. New York: Chelsea House, 2006.

———. *Who Wrote That? R.L. Stine*. New York: Chelsea House, 2006.

———. *Who Wrote That? Will Hobbs*. New York: Chelsea House, 2005.

Morano, Marylou. *Who Wrote That? Ann M. Martin*. New York: Chelsea House, 2005.

Peltak, Jennifer. *Who Wrote That? Beverly Cleary.* New York: Chelsea House, 2005.

Sexton, Colleen A. *J.K. Rowling.* Minneapolis, Minn.: Twentyfirst Century Books, 2006.

Speaker-Yuan, Margaret. *Who Wrote That? Avi.* New York: Chelsea House, 2005.

———. *Who Wrote That? Beatrix Potter.* New York: Chelsea House, 2005.

WITH THE EXPERTS

Association of Talent Agents
9255 Sunset Boulevard, Suite 930
Los Angeles, CA 90069-3317
http://www.agentassociation.com

Association of Authors' Representatives
676A Ninth Avenue, Suite 312
New York, NY 10036-3602
http://www.aar-online.org

GET ACQUAINTED

David Hendin, Literary Agent

CAREER PATH

CHILDHOOD ASPIRATION: To be a doctor or a baseball player.

FIRST JOB: Performed magic shows from age nine through college.

CURRENT JOB: Literary agent.

FROM TEACHER TO JOURNALIST

David Hendin grew up in St. Louis. After he graduated from college, Hendin found that teachers were needed in Israel, and he volunteered to teach high school biology. He was there one year, returned to the United States, received his master's degree in journalism, and went to work as a newspaper syndicated feature writer for United Feature Syndicate. (There are five major syndicates. Look at the small print at the beginning or end of stories in your local newspaper and you'll see if an article, editorial, or comic strip is syndicated.)

Hendin was a syndicated feature writer for 10 years, covering health, science, and the environment. When the first Earth Day was celebrated, Hendin wrote many columns about what was happening across the country. Environmental issues became more and more important, and Hendin was involved in bringing those stories to the American public. He also wrote about many medical advances during his journalistic career.

FROM WRITER TO MANAGER

Hendin moved into the management side of United Feature Syndicate and advanced to the positions of president of the book publishing division and senior vice president of the newspaper syndicate. While in those positions, he learned the art of negotiating contracts and had the opportunity to syndicate numerous famous comic strips and columnists.

GARFIELD WHO?

That crazy cat Garfield is in the comics partly because of Hendin. The comic strip was syndicated under his direction. Where would the world of business be without Dilbert? Hendin also signed that strip. And how good are your manners? Read "Miss Manners" (Judith Martin) to see how you're doing! That column was also syndicated by Hendin. At the time he signed "Miss Manners," there were no real etiquette columns in newspapers, and people said it wouldn't work. "Garfield" and "Dilbert" were not big successes in the beginning either. But look how popular they are now.

OUT ON HIS OWN

Hendin left the newspaper and book publishing company and started his own literary agency. The experience he gained during his career in the syndication business was invaluable in his new venture.

Now Hendin works with writers and artists to help them develop their work and market it to publishers or newspaper syndicates. He represents writers and cartoonists and deals in both fiction and nonfiction. He has some 50 clients. Judith Martin (Miss Manners) happens to be one of them. He also represents Guy and Brad Gilchrist, the creators of the "Nancy and Sluggo" cartoon strip. Dr. Abraham Twerski, a rabbi and psychiatrist who writes inspirational and self-help books, is also a client.

A FEW WORDS OF ADVICE

Hendin's advice for anyone who wants to enter the writing field is simple. He says, "Read a lot; write a lot. Read some more; write some more. Do interesting things and then write about them."

Hendin says that, throughout life, things always happen when least expected. If something is not an immediate success, stick to it, and you may be surprised at how successful it might be later on. Remember Garfield, Dilbert, and Miss Manners.

Paralegal

SKILL SET

✔ COMPUTERS

✔ WRITING

✔ ADVENTURE

SHORTCUTS

GO visit your state legislature to see how laws are made.

READ John Grisham's books *The Rainmaker* (New York: Doubleday, 1995) or *The Firm* (New York: Doubleday, 1991). Both books feature some rather colorful paralegal talent.

TRY following news coverage of a big legal battle.

WHAT IS A PARALEGAL?

Paralegals, or legal assistants, work with lawyers to prepare information for legal cases. Paralegals research relevant information, organize facts and materials, and prepare comprehensive reports that are used by lawyers to prepare for lawsuits, trials, and other legal actions. In addition, more experienced paralegals may help prepare legal arguments, draft pleadings and motions to be filed in court, obtain affidavits, and assist lawyers in other ways. In fact, paralegals do many of the same types of tasks that lawyers do, with a few notable exceptions. Paralegals cannot set legal fees, they cannot offer legal advice, and they cannot try cases in court.

Paralegal work requires an ability to conduct thorough research and to communicate the findings in a professional, organized way. As these documents can be very complex, paralegals must use good judgment in deciding how much information should be included in order to give a complete representation of the issue being explored. In addition to using law libraries, paralegals also use online legal research databases to make sure that they fully investigate every bit of information that might be relevant to a case. Speaking of investigation, paralegals often must get pretty creative in finding ways to track down all the facts in a case.

There are several ways to obtain the training needed to become a paralegal. Many colleges and universities offer two- to four-year paralegal programs that result in earning either an associate's degree or bachelor's degree. There are also certification courses that can be earned in a matter of months. This flexibility allows for some creative career-building options. For instance, one person may earn a four-year liberal arts degree and then earn a paralegal certificate. Another may choose to earn the certificate first, get experience in the legal profession, and pursue additional education later. Others start working in a law office as a clerk or legal secretary and are promoted as they gain the necessary on-the-job training and experience. Some paralegals even go on to become lawyers.

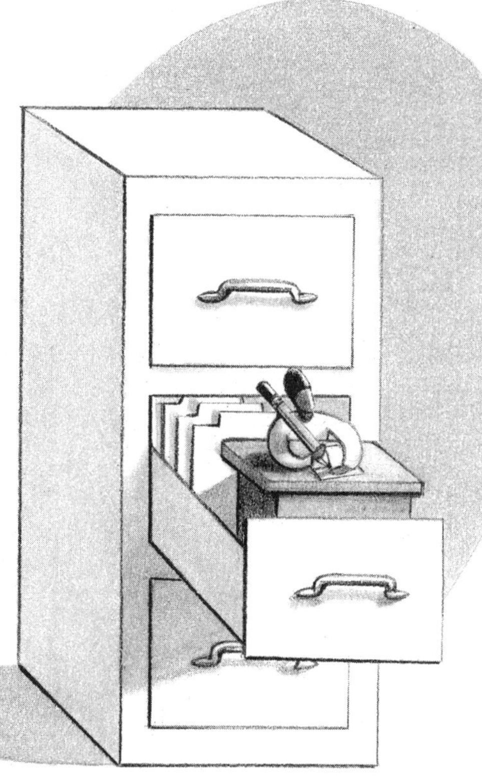

Although it is not an absolute requirement, some paralegals find it to their advantage to become certified either by the National Association of Legal Assistants or the National Federation of Paralegal Associations. As in other careers, making a commitment to professionalism and learning as much as possible can only help advance your career.

Paralegals may specialize in a particular type of law such as corporate law, criminal law, sports and entertainment law, constitutional law, or environmental law. They may work for attorneys in large legal firms or small law offices as well as for government and community service agencies. Legal departments in corporations also hire paralegals. A paralegal career offers the opportunity to gain valuable technical writing skills while working in a very professional and highly specialized field.

TRY IT OUT

GET STUCK IN THE MIDDLE

Many schools organize peer mediation programs where students are trained to help other students work out disagreements. This can be an excellent way to experience justice in action. Talk to your school counselor or student council sponsor about peer mediation programs in your school district.

LEGISLATIVE SLEUTH

Get on the trail of some of the government's latest legislative issues. Go online to Thomas (as in Thomas Jefferson, the official legislative Web site of the Library of Congress) at http://thomas.loc.gov to find up-to-the-minute information about bills under consideration by the U.S. House of Representatives and U.S. Senate. Click on "Yesterday in Congress" or "On the House Floor Now" to find summaries of bills. Choose one that interests you and click on the links to see a full copy of the proposed legislation.

Go through the bill and highlight any legal terms or "legalese" that you are unfamiliar with. Once you have a sense of what the bill is all about, write a brief summary using more kid-friendly language.

SPEND THE DAY IN COURT

The next time you have a day off from school, make arrangements to sit in on the proceedings in a courtroom. Whether it's juvenile court, traffic court, or the site of a major legal proceeding, it's sure to be an eye-opening experience.

Make a list of the types of cases presented and keep tabs on the verdicts.

HOW LAWS WORK

Go online to some of these very informative Web sites to learn a little more about how the U.S. legal system works:

- Ben's Guide to the U.S. Government for Kids at http://bensguide.gpo.gov/6-8/index.html
- Bill of Rights for Kids at http://www.njsbf.com/njsbf/student/billofrights.pdf
- Kids in the House at http://clerkkids.house.gov
- Law for Kids at http://www.lawforkids.org
- Legal Glossary for Kids at http://www.leg.state.fl.us/kids/glossary
- All About Court at http://www.factmonster.com/ipka/A0769420.html
- The Legislative Process at http://congress.indiana.edu/learn_about/topic/legislative_process.php

 AT THE LIBRARY

LEGAL BRIEFS

Paralegals rely on a well-informed knowledge of important laws to do their job. The following books, all from a series called *Great Supreme Court Decisions*, introduce some of the most important laws in American history:

Hitchcock, Susan Tyler. *Roe v. Wade: Protecting a Woman's Right to Choose*. New York: Chelsea House, 2006.

McNeese, Tim. *Brown v. Board of Education: Integrating America's Schools*. New York: Chelsea House, 2006.

———. *Dred Scott v. Sandford: The Pursuit of Freedom*. New York: Chelsea House, 2006.

———. *Plessy v. Ferguson: Separate But Equal*. New York: Chelsea House, 2006.

———. *Regents of the University of California v. Bakke: American Education and Affirmative Action*. New York: Chelsea House, 2007.

Mountjoy, Shane. *Engel v. Vitale: School Prayer and the Establishment Clause*. New York: Chelsea House, 2006.
———. *Marbury v. Madison: Establishing Supreme Court Power*. New York: Chelsea House, 2006.
Roensch, Greg, and Tim McNeese. *Furman v. Georgia: Cruel and Unusual Punishment*. New York: Chelsea. House, 2007.
Vanmeter, Larry A. *Miranda v. Arizona: The Rights of the Accused*. New York: Chelsea House, 2006.

WITH THE EXPERTS

American Association for Paralegal Education
19 Mantua Road
Mount Royal, NJ 08061-1006
http://www.aafpe.org

American Bar Association
321 North Clark Street
Chicago, IL 60610-7598
http://www.abanet.org

National Federation of Paralegal Associations
PO Box 2016
Edmonds, WA 98020-9516
http://www.paralegals.org

National Paralegal Association
Box 406
Solebury, PA 18963-0406
http://www.nationalparalegal.org

GET ACQUAINTED

Kimberle English, Paralegal

CAREER PATH

CHILDHOOD ASPIRATION: To be a flight attendant.

FIRST JOB: Working at a women's clothes store.

CURRENT JOB: Paralegal with Holland and Hart, (http://www.hollandhart.com), a large western law firm.

A FEW DETOURS ALONG THE WAY

When Kimberle English was in high school, she got involved with Distributive Education Clubs of America (DECA). In this program, she and several of her friends had fun learning about real life and various careers. In the process, she discovered that she had a real interest in the law. After she graduated, she enrolled in a community college with every intention of going on to law school and becoming an attorney. Two years later she had earned an associate's degree, but her plan got left behind when she got married and had two children.

As it turns out, her husband left soon after the second child was born. English found herself with two children, few job skills, and no means of support for her young family. English soon found herself homeless and had to depend on public assistance to get through that tough period in her life.

Fortunately, she still had the desire to go into the legal profession, but with two children to raise and support, several years of law school was out of the question. She found, however, that the associate's degree she'd earned earlier served her well when she enrolled in a training program for paralegals. English was able to skip several courses by passing some tests and managed to finish the two-year program in little more than a year.

A FRESH START

One of English's professors recommended her to a placement firm that specialized in paralegal work. Since she had graduated at the top of the class, English had no trouble finding lawyers who were willing to assign temporary special projects to her. Sometimes the work was as simple as transcribing dictation tapes (lots of typing!) or filing. One project required her to organize hundreds of boxes of documents for a huge court case involving the firm.

English worked in various law firms on a temporary basis until one offered her a full-time position. She eventually moved into her present position and really enjoys the opportunity to work on some of the more challenging aspects of paralegal work.

THE THRILL OF THE CHASE

English says that her favorite part of the job is the research. Each case is different, and she enjoys seeking out all the relevant information she can find. She finds that giving careful attention to every detail pays off, and she takes satisfaction in knowing that the result of her meticulous preparation can help clients win their legal battles.

In her current position, English mostly specializes in cases having to do with personal injury litigation and business litigation. But she also has worked on cases that involved product liability, wrongful death, and environmental litigation.

THE COMMA LADY

No offense intended, but English has discovered that most attorneys need help expressing themselves. The attorneys she works with have come to rely on her command of grammar, punctuation, and other basics of written communication to make their sometimes brilliant legal insights read intelligently. One of the grammatically challenged lawyers has dubbed her "the comma lady."

As she's gained more experience as a paralegal, English has been surprised to discover how much writing the job requires. She spends a lot of time writing discoveries, communicating with clients, and drafting pleadings for the partners. She also enjoys writing articles for the Idaho paralegal association.

A HAPPY ENDING

Even though her original career ambitions got derailed by life's circumstances, English says that paralegal work is the best choice for her right now. She's still busy raising her children and would find it difficult to juggle being a single mother with all the responsibilities of being a lawyer. For now, being a paralegal offers the best of both worlds. She does much of the same kinds of interesting work that lawyers do, but she is able to sleep better at night knowing that the attorney has the ultimate responsibility.

Publicist

SKILL SET

- ✔ ADVENTURE
- ✔ TALKING
- ✔ WRITING

SHORTCUTS

GO to the movies, a concert, or a sports event and take note of all the promotional materials that are used to set the tone and bring in an audience.

READ the feature section of a major newspaper. You can bet that many of the articles about celebrities and new products got there as a result of a publicist's creative efforts.

TRY helping promote the next school dance or football game.

WHAT IS A PUBLICIST?

Having one's own publicist is the one thing that every big rock star, actor, author, pro athlete, and politician have in common. Publicists are public relations specialists who work to keep their clients' names in the news. Of course, it is generally preferred that their clients' names be associated with good news. But a skilled publicist will know how to put a positive spin on the worst of circumstances as well.

Publicists help their famous clients stay famous by working with the media to keep them informed about noteworthy (or at least interesting) events. They do this by sending press releases and kits to carefully selected media people. Perhaps most important, they do it by maintaining friendly relationships with these people. This is a career in which *what* you know may be important but *who* you know is crucial. The most successful publicists take the time to nurture good relationships and earn the trust of the people who report the news by dealing with them professionally and with integrity.

Publicists may work for a public relations firm, a publishing house, a film studio, a major corporation, or a sports team. Publicists with experience and good contacts are just as likely to work independently, setting up their own business and

representing any number of clients. They plan and implement publicity campaigns to get media attention for their clients.

While the work can be as varied as the personalities that publicists represent, there are several tasks that characterize the profession. For instance, you can count on publicists having a comprehensive press kit and media file for each of their clients. The press kit would include some basic ingredients such as a brief biography, photographs, and news clips about the client. Press kits are sent out along with a press release whenever there is a major event such as the release of a new movie or book or as part of a publicity campaign. Key to getting the coverage that's desired is writing effective press releases that, while subtlely self-serving, contain information an audience would want. Television and radio talk shows are other media sources that publicists work with to schedule spots for their clients.

In addition to actively seeking media coverage, a publicist may also handle inquiries from the media as a spokesperson for clients. This is particularly true in times of trouble when the publicist will work with the client to prepare a statement that represents the client's views on a matter and provide it to the media. This can be a useful way to satisfy curiosity while helping to maintain at least a semblance of privacy for the client.

Publicists may also arrange news conferences for clients to talk directly with the press, schedule private interviews with specific reporters, arrange photo opportunities for the press to get pictures of their clients, and plan special events such as opening night parties to gain added exposure for their clients. Media files are kept to track the success of publicity campaigns, and they contain clippings about their clients from newspapers and magazines all over the world. To keep a client or a job, publicists must prove their effectiveness by consistently getting their client's name in print or over the airwaves. Of course, all of these activities require very detailed planning and coordination with reporters. That part of the job keeps publicists busy on the phone.

If the publicist works for a publishing house or represents a notable author, he or she may also be responsible for scheduling author tours. This can be a rather complex undertaking that involves setting up interviews and special events in several cities across the country. The publicist is often responsible for planning the entire itinerary down to the smallest detail—including travel, lodging, and arranging for special meals. And the publicist's work begins long before the author arrives in a given city because the publicist must create an awareness of the authors and their latest books prior to the visit. One important part of this process is sending out review copies to book reviewers and feature writers of carefully selected newspapers and other appropriate publications.

Publicity is sought by any business to keep its name and products in full view of the buying public. Public relations is generally an important part of a company's overall marketing strategy. Think about it. Can you imagine how much it would cost to buy space to advertise your business on the front page of a national newspaper? Forget the specifics—you can be sure that it would cost a lot. What if you could get that space for the cost of a postage stamp and a few sheets of paper for a press release? Now you know why publicity and the people who know how to get it can be so valuable.

Publicists generally have earned a college degree in a field such as communications, public relations, journalism, or business. Seldom, if ever, do they start their careers by representing big Hollywood stars. Instead, they begin by working in a public relations firm or publishing house, photocopying and stuffing envelopes, while they learn techniques and perfect their skills.

TRY IT OUT

CLUB PR

Be on the lookout for groups in your school that could use some good public relations (PR)—maybe a sports team or an after-school club. Think of some newsworthy nugget of information and prepare a press kit to submit to the school or community newspaper. Perhaps your school band just got new uniforms or someone on the cross-country team broke a school record at the last meet.

Whatever the news, here are some things to include in your press kit: a press release that has a catchy headline, an interesting "hook" to get the reader interested in the story, and enough details to answer the who, what, where, when, why, and how questions that inquiring reporters everywhere will want answered; photographs of the event or the people featured in the story; and any other background materials that would make it easy for the newspaper editor to run your story in the next edition.

A VOTE FOR PUBLICITY

School elections are another good place to put your skills as a publicist to the test. Volunteer to help a candidate spread the word about his or her campaign. Start by drawing up a plan that includes all the ideas you can think of for getting out the vote in the candidate's favor. Look at all the resources—publicity materials such as posters, special events that he or she can participate in, and other means to present his or her platform.

If you find that you enjoy the political process, don't stop with school elections. Volunteer to help work on any local campaign. Anyone running for public office—from a town council member to president of the United States—needs publicity. Find out how you can help get the word out about a good candidate.

CHARACTER STUDIES

Your favorite animated or cartoon character has just hired you to be his or her publicist. They want you to put together a poster to publicize their best work. Go online to find resources at cartoon-friendly Web sites such as:

- Cartoon Network at http://www.cartoonnetwork.com
- Disney at http://www.disney.com
- Nickelodeon at http://www.nick.com

ON THE WEB

FREE ADVERTISING

The Internet is the newest frontier for businesses looking to promote themselves. Here you'll find plenty of outright selling of goods, but if you look close enough, you'll also see some more subtle selling of a corporate image. Companies of all sizes are finding the Internet to be an effective way to promote their businesses with the type of information and activities that is the mainstay of good publicity. Quite often, companies gain name recognition by providing a useful service online. See for yourself how effective this public relations strategy can be by visiting the following sites.

http://www.gap.com
http://www.hersheys.com

http://www.universalstudios.com
http://www2.kelloggs.com
http://www.rbk.com

 AT THE LIBRARY

PEOPLE IN THE NEWS

Read up on some celebrities and other news makers in books such as:

Abraham, Philip. *Tobey Maguire.* Danbury, Conn.: Scholastic Library, 2003.
Beyer, Mark. *Frankie Muniz.* Danbury, Conn.: Scholastic Library, 2002.
Fingeroth, Danny. *Liv Tyler.* Danbury, Conn.: Scholastic Library, 2003.
Galens, Judy and Allison McNeill. *Newsmakers (Volumes 1 – 6).* Farmington Hills, Mich.: UXL, 2005.
Laslo, Cynthia. *Brandy.* Danbury, Conn. Scholastic Library, 2000.
McCracken, Kristen. *Leonardo DiCaprio.* Danbury, Conn.: Scholastic Library, 2000.
Rivera, Ursula. *Reese Witherspoon.* Danbury, Conn.: Scholastic Library, 2003.
———. *Shakira.* Danbury, Conn.: Scholastic Library, 2003.

WITH THE EXPERTS

Publishers Marketing Association
627 Aviation Way
Manhattan Beach, CA 90266-7107
http://www.pma-online.org

Publishers' Publicity Association
1745 Broadway
New York, NY 10019-4305
http://www.publisherspublicity.org

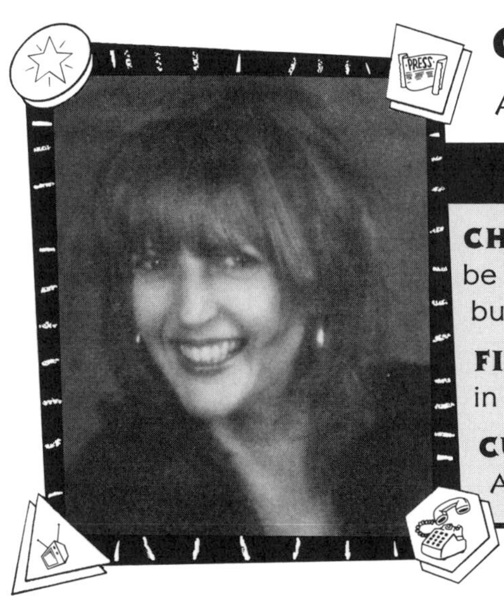

GET ACQUAINTED

Ann Flower, Publicist

CAREER PATH

CHILDHOOD ASPIRATION: To be an ecologist or start her own business.

FIRST JOB: Curatorial assistant in an art gallery.

CURRENT JOB: President of Ann Flower Communications.

EXPERIENCE COUNTS

Ann Flower is the daughter of two artists. Her only sister is an artist too. She says it seemed as though her parents and her sister were born knowing what to do. Their talents were recognized very early, so they went to art school and became artists. It wasn't so easy for Flower. She had many interests, could do several things fairly well, and was what you might call a "jack of all trades."

After Flower graduated from high school, she went to school in Europe for a year and liked it so well that she stayed for a while just to goof off and see the world. She came back to the United States and continued her schooling for a couple of years before taking off for Australia, where she had a job working for an American company. She then proceeded to work in a variety of fascinating jobs that prepared her for the work she is doing now.

There's a lesson to be learned from Flower's story. She admits, with a bit of hesitation, the she never finished her college education. On one hand, she regrets it. On the other hand, all the experience she gained from traveling and working helped prepare her for the work she's doing now.

There are some things you can't learn in a book, and it turns out that her varied interests and talents were exactly what she needed to succeed as a public relations professional. Of course, she is quick to point out that her approach was unusual and wouldn't work for everyone.

AN ACCIDENTAL ENCOUNTER WITH PR

Flower found a career in public relations as a result of working as an assistant for a television producer. He told her about a job opening for a nonprofit organization called AmFAR (American Foundation for AIDS Research). She was intrigued by the idea of giving something back to the world, so she applied for the job and was hired to help organize fundraising events. The job involved working with various public relations agencies to stage and publicize the events. That's where she discovered that public relations was a profession that really fit her eclectic background.

HOBNOBBING WITH CELEBRITIES

Her next career stop was handling public relations at a hotel in Santa Monica, California. Then she moved on to what she calls the ultimate hotel PR job at the prestigious Beverly Wilshire Hotel in Los Angeles, the site for the movie *Pretty Woman*. She said the job was fascinating, exciting, and busy—very busy. It seemed as though everyone who was anyone walked through the doors of that hotel. She had the opportunity to meet famous movie stars such as Michael Jackson, Elizabeth Taylor, and the late Jimmy Stewart. She was most intrigued by all the world leaders who came her way, including Nelson Mandela, Margaret Thatcher, Hillary Clinton, Prince Andrew, Sarah Ferguson, and the Dalai Lama.

ON HER OWN

Flower's expertise in hotel public relations landed her a position as vice president of the hospitality division for a public relations firm. She worked with a variety of clients until a few of her favorites talked her into starting her own agency so that she could give them more of her time.

She now handles publicity for clients as diverse as hotels in Mexico, California, and Canada, high-tech consumer products, and the convention and visitors bureau for a seaside community, as well as special events like home shows, Scottish Highland Games, and art fairs. As different as the clients may be, her goal for all of them is the same: to find creative ways to expose them and their products to consumers. Achieving this goal may involve anything from having photographs of the client's products used in a magazine article to arranging a profile about the charitable activities of one of her clients.

VIRTUES OF THE SUCCESSFUL PUBLICIST

Flower says that you need two things to succeed in public relations: energy (lots of it) and patience (tons of it). When you are working for high-profile clients, the pace can run you ragged with the phone ringing constantly and events, interviews, and photo shoots keeping you hopping. It takes a high level of energy to keep up.

Patience comes into play with the realization that good publicity doesn't come overnight. Flower says that it has taken up to a year to get some of her story ideas in print. Patience has paid off for Flower with major hits in publications such as *People* magazine, *USA Today*, and the *New York Times*. Publications like this get her clients' names in front of millions of people—making it well worth the wait.

Talk Show Producer

SKILL SET

- ✔ ADVENTURE
- ✔ TALKING
- ✔ WRITING

SHORTCUTS

GO sit in the audience of a television or radio talk show and watch how a show comes together.

READ *Teen People* online at http://www.teenpeople.com to find out who's talking about whom in showbiz.

TRY making a list of ideas that would be interesting to discuss in a talk show format.

WHAT IS A TALK SHOW PRODUCER?

A talk show producer's work is quite similar to a newspaper or magazine editor's work. They are responsible for putting together an interesting variety of stories and information in a limited amount of space. There are three notable differences, however.

First, a talk show producer works with time limitations as opposed to space limitations. A talk show may consist of as much as an hour of airtime or as little as a five-second sound bite. Another difference is that although a talk show producer starts with written stories and pictures much like a newspaper editor, he or she must also work with the added dimensions of voices, personalities, and in the case of television, cameras and three-dimensional, moving graphics. The final difference, and it can be a big one, is that a talk show producer's work is often broadcast before a live audience. Producers don't have the luxury of editing their words and fixing mistakes. It's all there in living color!

All these ingredients make for a fast-paced and stimulating work environment that is ideal for writers who have lots of creative ideas, can think fast on their feet, and can make sound decisions about what's news and what's not. Good taste in developing stories that are appropriate for the general public's viewing is another increasingly appreciated skill for talk show producers.

As you might expect, writing for a talk show can be quite different from writing for other formats. The copy must be concise, lively, and easily communicated verbally. Scripts must be tight and writers must consistently meet the challenge of effectively condensing major newsworthy events into 10- to 20-second stories.

Depending on the format of a show, a producer may be responsible for writing stories and putting together shows about the day's news, special edition news digests, documentaries about topics of interest to broad viewing audiences, promotional spots, and/or interviews with celebrities and other news makers.

In addition to producing television and radio talk shows, talented writers may find opportunity in the growing audio book publishing industry. Here a producer must condense popular fiction or nonfiction books by about 60 percent so that the book can be read within the two- or three-hour timeframe that is standard for such products. The trick is that this must be achieved without sacrificing any of the most important aspects of the book—the characters, plot, setting—or the natural "voice" of the original book. It requires a process that goes a lot like this: Read the book, reread the book, write, cut, rewrite, cut, reread, cut some more, and so on.

Writers who want to produce television or radio talk shows or audio books would be well served by good training in a field such as broadcast journalism or communications. A college degree and experience at any level are helpful keys for getting started. More opportunities are to be found at smaller stations in smaller cities. Assignments for shows such as *The Ellen DeGeneres Show* and *Good Morning America* go to producers and writers who have proven themselves in smaller arenas and gained the skills and professional savvy necessary for making it in the big time.

LIVE AT SIX

Take a typical day at school and make a list of all the noteworthy events. Go through the list and choose the five most important events. Write a news report that includes these stories in order of importance. Keep the language clear and concise but make sure the story highlights the most important aspects of the event. Your coverage should be complete enough that anyone could understand the significance of the story. Don't forget the weather and sports! Use a video camera or tape recorder to capture the results.

CUT TO THE CHASE

Pick a chapter from a favorite book, or find a good children's book—something interesting and of reasonable length. Your job is to rewrite the chapter or book, cutting it by at least 25 percent so that it can be read as a book on tape. See what you can do to tighten things up without losing the original flavor and intent of the book's author. When you've finished, read the results into a tape recorder. Play the tape and see what you think.

NEWS IN A NUTSHELL

Listen to the evening news for an introduction to the skill of writing sound bites. Sound bites are quotes or explanations that somehow manage to conceptualize an entire subject or event in a matter of seconds. Good sound bites may be brief, but they are packed with memorable information. Politicians tend to be highly skilled in the art of sound bites. Pay attention to the way they describe legislative bills or issues on the newscast.

Now, think about something that has happened recently at school or in your community. See if you can come up with a clever sentence or two to explain it.

ON THE WEB

PRODUCER FOR A DAY

Pretend that you are the producer of your favorite television or radio talk show. Dr. Phil? Regis and Kelly? David Letterman? The line-up for tonight's show has completely fallen apart. You have to come up with a new show—now! Think of what topics and guests you'd put together for an entertaining show.

Get some ideas by checking out the actual line-ups of some of your favorite talk shows. Here are some Web addresses for starters.

- *CBS Early Show* at http://www.cbsnews.com/sections/earlyshow/main500202.shtml
- *Late Night with David Letterman* at http://www.cbs.com/latenight/lateshow
- *Dr. Phil* at http://www.drphil.com
- *Good Morning America* at http://abcnews.go.com/GMA
- *The Tonight Show with Jay Leno* at http://www.nbc.com/The_Tonight_Show_with_Jay_Leno
- *The Oprah Winfrey Show* at http://www2.oprah.com

- *Live with Regis and Kelly* at http://bventertainment.go.com/tv/buenavista/regisandkelly/index.html
- *The Today Show* at http://www.msnbc.msn.com/id/3032633

AT THE LIBRARY

SPOTLIGHT ON PEOPLE

Imagine what it would be like to interview some of the following notable people. Read up on their backgrounds and make a list of five questions you'd ask each person if you were a talk show host.

Brandon, Karen. *People in the News: Arnold Schwarzenegger.* Farmington Hills, Mich.: Lucent Books, 2004.

Devaney, Sherri and Mark Devaney. *People in the News: Barack Obama.* Farmington Hills, Mich.: Lucent Books, 2006.

Epstein, Dwayne. *People in the News: Adam Sandler.* Farmington Hills, Mich.: Lucent Books, 2004.

Lynette, Rachel. *People in the News: Angelina Jolie.* Farmington Hills, Mich.: Lucent Books, 2006.

Steffens, Bradley. *People in the News: J.K. Rowling.* Farmington Hills, Mich.: Lucent Books, 2006.

Uschan, Michael V. *People in the News: Tiger Woods.* Farmington Hills, Mich.: Lucent Books, 1999.

Wukovits, John F. *People in the News: Ben Affleck.* Farmington Hills, Mich.: Lucent Books, 2004.

———. *People in the News: Colin Powell.* Farmington Hills, Mich.: Lucent Books, 1999.

WITH THE EXPERTS

Audio Publishers Association
191 Clarksville Road
Princeton Junction, NJ 08550-5303
http://www.audiopub.org

National Association of Radio Talk Show Hosts
2791 South Buffalo Drive
Las Vegas, NV 89117-2927
http://www.talkshowhosts.com

Producers Guild of America
8530 Wilshire Boulevard, Suite 450
Beverly Hills, CA 90211-3115
http://www.producersguild.org

Society of Professional Audio Recording Services
Nine Music Square South, Suite 222
Nashville, TN 37203-3211
http://www.spars.com

GET ACQUAINTED

Tom Giesen, Television Producer

CAREER PATH

CHILDHOOD ASPIRATION: To be a writer.

FIRST JOB: Dishwasher at The Bum Steer in Waterloo, Iowa.

CURRENT JOB: Executive producer with High Noon Entertainment.

GO FOR THE GOAL

Ever since seeing the movie *All the President's Men* at the age of 13, Tom Giesen wanted to be a reporter. He attended parochial schools in Iowa and graduated from the University of Iowa with a degree in journalism. He also took television production classes and participated in theater productions.

LEARNING THE ROPES

Even though Giesen thought he wanted to be a television reporter, he decided that he had "more of a face for radio." He moved to Bloomington, Indiana, where he was hired to do on-air promotions in a small television market. He did a little bit of everything—from writing and creating graphics to producing and appearing on the air. Getting the chance to do it all showed him that he really liked writing and working behind the scenes best.

One of the funniest things that happened to Giesen during his stint in Indiana was being upstaged by a pig while working on a show called *Live from the Monroe County Fair.* He was interviewing a young 4-H girl who had shown the prize pig. The pig liked plastic and wrapped himself in the microphone cord and took the microphone from Giesen. The pig finally dropped the microphone and the show went on!

ON TO BIGGER AND BETTER THINGS

Giesen moved on to Minnesota where he was a television news editor with the working hours of midnight to 9:00 A.M. (That doesn't do much for one's social life, does it?) He produced *Good Company,* a very popular talk show hosted by a husband and wife team and similar to *Live with Regis and Kathie Lee.* At the time, *Good Company* was the highest rated local show in the country. The success of that show resulted in a call from a major television station in Colorado.

NEXT ON THE AGENDA

Giesen became writer and producer for *Good Afternoon, Colorado,* another very popular news and talk show. He was producer of that show for two years. During one of the shows, author Tony Hillerman's book *Sacred Clowns* was being reviewed. Giesen was in charge of the TelePrompTer (that's what the TV personality reads from). He accidentally wrote *Scared Clowns* rather than Sacred Clowns. Hillerman had fun kidding Giesen on air—something Giesen hasn't forgotten yet!

ON A ROLL

Finally, the more creative end of television beckoned, and Giesen has been a freelance writer and producer for the past several years. During that time he produced a crafts and antiques show for the Discovery Channel and 200 four-minute features for Discovery. He has written and produced business shows that aired on the Knowledge TV channel and several kids' shows. One, a show about video games, called *Twitch*, was very popular.

Now he is an executive with High Noon Entertainment, a television production company known for capturing fascinating stories of everyday people in alternative and reality shows. According to his company's Web site, "High Noon melds contemporary pop culture with heartfelt drama to connect with the dreams, aspirations and interests of the mainstream American viewing audience."

Giesen currently produces the series *Food Network Challenge* for the Food Network as well as HGTV's popular series *If Walls Could Talk* and *Designer Finals*. Over the years, Giesen has worked on hundreds of hours of programming, including the Food Network series *All-American Festivals*, and HGTV's *Hey Remember*, *A Place to Call Home*, and *Christmas Castles*.

JUST WRITE IT

Giesen says if you want to write, you need to understand grammar and "be a great speller" (even when you have spell check on your computer). He believes in a casual style of writing, that is, writing the way people talk. Engage people with your writing, and help them understand your message. They need to "hear" what you're saying. Be interesting, be funny, and always meet your deadlines!

If you like to write, get involved in your school newspaper or yearbook production. Write as much as you can. Write so that people want to read or listen to what you write.

MAKE A WRITING DETOUR!

It's pretty amazing to think about all the ways you could put your interest in writing to work. The following lists include dozens of writing careers, and they barely scratch the surface of all the possibilities. These ideas are loosely grouped in categories to help you narrow down specific interest areas. Use them as a starting point to search out the best spot for your interests and abilities.

To make the most of this phase of your exploration, draw up a list of the ideas that you'd like to learn more about. Chances are there are at least three you've never heard of before. Look them up in a career encyclopedia and get acquainted with more possibilities for your future!

When you come across a particularly intriguing occupation, use the form on page 166 to record your discoveries.

A WORLD OF WRITING CAREERS

Write your way to success in some of the following careers.

A WAY WITH WORDS

These careers are for wordsmiths who have something to say and know how to say it.

cartoonist
catalog copywriter
children's book author
freelance writer
ghostwriter
greeting card writer
headline writer
journalist
newspaper columnist
novelist
playwright
poet
screenwriter
speechwriter
technical writer
television series writer
textbook writer
travel writer

THE BIG PICTURE

These careers require an ear for good and powerful language and a knack for managing the many details associated with producing books and other media products. A flair for writing in ways suitable to specific types of projects is also essential.

acquisitions editor
audio book producer
CD-ROM editor
children's book editor
computer game designer
database editor
desktop publisher
educational software editor
electronic publication specialist
encyclopedia editor
features editor
magazine editor
multimedia producer
online editor
TV producer
webmaster

NITTY-GRITTY DETAILS

People who do the following jobs often save other writers from seeing their embarrassing mistakes in print. These jobs involve some of the quality assurance aspects of writing and publishing.

abstractor
copy editor
dictionary editor
grammarian
indexer
proofreader
researcher

FAST AND FURIOUS

Tight deadlines and fast-paced writing demands are common ingredients of the following career ideas.

assignment editor
bureau chief
city editor
news anchor
news service correspondent
press secretary
public information officer
radio newscaster
reporter
stringer
wire service correspondent

IN OTHER WORDS

Teaching, analyzing, critiquing, or interpreting other people's writing is central to the following careers.

book reviewer
book buyer
critic
English teacher
English as a Second Language (ESL) teacher
journalism teacher
translator

IN THE WORD BUSINESS

While writing is only a part of the following occupations, it plays a big part, and good writing and communication skills are essential for success in these fields.

communications consultant
community affairs director
consumer affairs specialist
corporate communications director
development director
employee publication specialist
fund-raiser
investor relations specialist
marketing manager
media buyer
media planner
nonprofit organization administrator
promotions manager
publicist
recruiter

It's been a fast-paced trip so far. Take a break, regroup, and look at all the progress you've made.

1st Stop: Discover
You discovered some personal interests and natural abilities that you can start building a career around.

2nd Stop: Explore
You've explored an exciting array of career opportunities in this field. You're now aware that your career can involve either a specialized area with educational requirements or that it can involve a practical application of writing skills with a minimum of training and experience.

At this point, you've found a couple careers that make you wonder "Is this a good option for me?" Now it's time to put it all together and make an informed, intelligent choice. It's time to get a sense of what it might be like to have a job like the one(s) you're considering. In other words, it's time to move on to step three and do a little experimenting with success.

3rd Stop: Experiment

By the time you finish this section, you'll have reached one of three points in the career planning process.

1. **Green light!** You found it. No need to look any further. This is the career for you. (This may happen to a lucky few. Don't worry if it hasn't happened yet for you. This whole process is about exploring options, experimenting with ideas, and, eventually, making the best choice for you.)
2. **Yellow light!** Close but not quite. You seem to be on the right path, but you haven't nailed things down for sure. (This is where many people your age end up, and it's a good place to be. You've learned what it takes to really check things out. Hang in there. Your time will come.)
3. **Red light!** Whoa! No doubt about it, this career just isn't for you. (Congratulations! Aren't you glad you found out now and not after you'd spent four years in college preparing for this career? Your next stop: Make a U-turn and start this process over with another career.)

Here's a sneak peek at what you'll be doing in the next section.

- First, you'll pick a favorite career idea (or two or three).
- Second, you'll link up with a whole world of great information about that career on the Internet (it's easier than you think).
- Third, you'll snoop around the library to find answers to the top 10 things you've just got to know about your future career.
- Fourth, you'll either write a letter or use the Internet to request information from a professional organization associated with this career.
- Fifth, you'll chat on the phone to conduct a telephone interview.

After all that you'll (finally!) be ready to put it all together in your very own Career Ideas for Kids career profile (see page 166).

Hang on to your hats and get ready to make tracks!

#1 NARROW DOWN YOUR CHOICES

You've been introduced to quite a few writing career ideas. You may also have some ideas of your own to add. Which ones appeal to you the most?

Write your top three choices in the spaces below. (Sorry if this is starting to sound like a broken record, but if this book does not belong to you, write your responses on a separate sheet of paper.)

1. ______________________________
2. ______________________________
3. ______________________________

#2 SURF THE NET

With the Internet, you have a world of information at your fingertips. The Internet has something for everyone, and it's getting easier to access all the time. An increasing number of libraries and schools are offering access to the Internet on their computers, or you may have a computer at home.

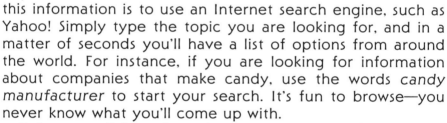

A typical career search will land everything from the latest news on developments in the field and course notes from universities to museum exhibits, interactive games, educational activities, and more. You just can't beat the timeliness or the variety of information available on the Web.

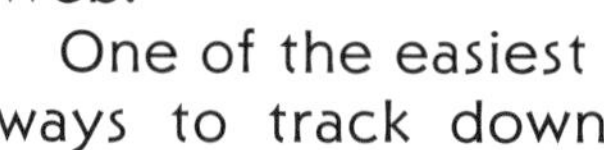

One of the easiest ways to track down this information is to use an Internet search engine, such as Yahoo! Simply type the topic you are looking for, and in a matter of seconds you'll have a list of options from around the world. For instance, if you are looking for information about companies that make candy, use the words *candy manufacturer* to start your search. It's fun to browse—you never know what you'll come up with.

Before you link up, keep in mind that many of these sites are geared toward professionals who are already working in a particular field. Some of the sites can get pretty technical. Just use the experience as a chance to nose around the field, hang out with the people who are tops in the field, and think about whether or not you'd like to be involved in a profession like that.

Specific sites to look for are the following:

Professional associations. Find out about what's happening in the field, conferences, journals, and other helpful tidbits.

Schools that specialize in this area. Many include research tools, introductory courses, and all kinds of interesting information.

Government agencies. Quite a few are going high-tech with lots of helpful resources.

Web sites hosted by experts in the field (this seems to be a popular hobby among many professionals). These Web sites are often as entertaining as they are informative.

If you're not sure where to go, just start clicking around. Sites often link to other sites. You may want to jot down notes about favorite sites. Sometimes you can even print information that isn't copyright protected; try the print option and see what happens.

Be prepared: Surfing the Internet can be an addicting habit! There is so much awesome information. It's a fun way to focus on your future.

Write the addresses of the three best Web sites that you find during your search in the space below (or on a separate sheet of paper if this book does not belong to you).

1. ______________________________

2. ______________________________

3. ______________________________

#3 SNOOP AT THE LIBRARY

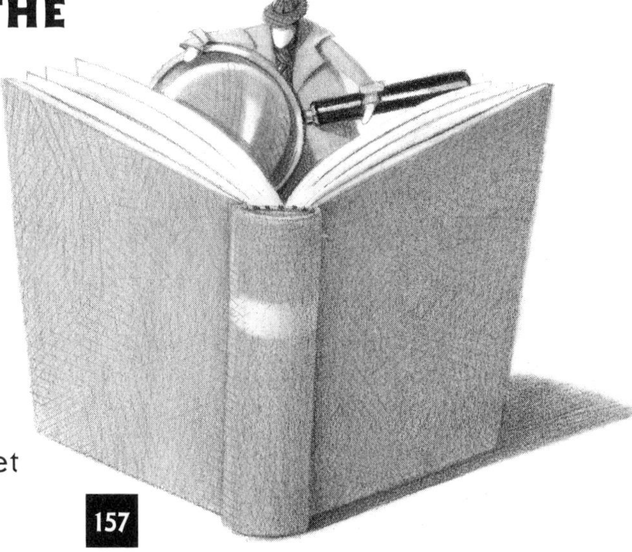

Take your list of favorite career ideas, a notebook, and a helpful adult with you to the library. When you get there, go to the reference section and ask the librarian to help you find books about careers. Most libraries will have at least one set of career encyclopedias. Some of the larger libraries may also have career information on CD-ROM.

Gather all the information you can and use it to answer the following questions in your notebook about each of the careers on your list. Make sure to ask for help if you get stuck.

TOP 10 THINGS YOU NEED TO KNOW ABOUT YOUR CAREER

1. What is the purpose of this job?

    ____

2. What kind of place is this type of work usually done in? For example, would I work mostly in a busy office, outdoors, or in a laboratory?

    ____

3. What kind of time is required to do this job? For instance, is the job usually performed during regular daytime business hours or do people work various shifts around the clock?

    ____

4. What kinds of tools are used to do this job?

    ____

5. In what ways does this job involve working with other people?

    ____

6. What kind of preparation does a person need to qualify for this job?

    ____

7. What kinds of skills and abilities are needed to be successful in this type of work?

   ____

8. What's a typical day on the job like?

   ____

   ____

9. How much money can I expect to earn as a beginner?

   ____

10. What kind of classes do I need to take in high school to get ready for this type of work?

   ____

#4 GET IN TOUCH WITH THE EXPERTS

One of the best places to find information about a particular career is a professional organization devoted especially to that career. After all, these organizations are full of the best and the brightest professionals working in that particular field. Who could possibly know more about how the work gets done? There are more than 450,000 organizations in the United States, so there is bound to be an association related to just about any career you can possibly imagine.

There are a couple ways you can find these organizations:

1. Look at the "Check It Out—With the Experts" list following a career you found especially interesting in the Take A Trip! section of this book.
2. Go online and use your favorite search engine (such as http://www.google.com or http://yahoo.com) to find professional associations related to a career you are

interested in. You might use the name of the career, plus the words *professional association* to start your search. You're likely to find lots of useful information online, so keep looking until you hit pay dirt.

3. Go to the reference section of your public library and ask the librarian to help you find a specific type of association in a reference book called *Encyclopedia of Associations* (Farmington Hills, Mich.: Thomson Gale) Or, if your library has access to it, the librarian may suggest using an online database called *Associations Unlimited* (Farmington Hills, Mich.: Thomson Gale).

Once you've tracked down a likely source of information, there are two ways to get in touch with a professional organization.

1. Send an e-mail.

   Most organizations include a "contact us" button on their Web sites. Sometimes this e-mail is directed to a webmaster or a customer service representative. An e-mail request might look something like this:

   Subject: Request for Information
   Date: 2/1/2008 3:18:41 PM Eastern Standard Time
   From: janedoe@mycomputer.com
   To: webmaster@candyloversassociation.org

   I am a fifth-grade student, and I am interested in learning more about careers for candy lovers. Would you please send me any information you have about what people do in your industry?

   Thank you very much.
   Jane Doe

2. Write a letter requesting information.

   Your letter should be either typed on a computer or written in your best handwriting. It should include the date, the complete address of the organization you are contacting, a salutation or greeting, a brief description of your request, and a signature. Make sure to include an address where the organization can reach you with a reply. Something like the following letter would work just fine.

> Dear Sir or Madam:
>
> I am a fifth-grade student, and I would like to learn more about what it is like to work in the candy lover profession. Would you please send me information about careers? My address is 456 Main Street, Anytown, USA 54321.
>
> Thank you very much.
>
> Sincerely,
> Jane Doe

Write the names and addresses of the professional organizations you discover on a separate sheet of paper.

#5 CHAT ON THE PHONE

Talking to a seasoned professional—someone who experiences the job day in and day out—can be a great way to get the inside story on what a career is all about. Fortunately for you, the experts in any career field can be as close as the nearest telephone.

Sure, it can be a bit scary calling up an adult whom you don't know. But two things are in your favor:

1. They can't see you. The worst thing they can do is hang up on you, so just relax and enjoy the conversation.
2. They'll probably be happy to talk to you about their job. In fact, most people will be flattered that you've called. If you happen to contact someone who seems reluctant to talk, thank them for their time and try someone else.

Here are a few pointers to help make your telephone interview a success:

- Mind your manners and speak clearly.
- Be respectful of their time and position.
- Be prepared with good questions and take notes as you talk.

One more common sense reminder: be careful about giving out your address and DO NOT arrange to meet anyone you don't know without your parents' supervision.

TRACKING DOWN CAREER EXPERTS

You might be wondering by now how to find someone to interview. Have no fear! It's easy if you're persistent. All you have to do is ask. Ask the right people and you'll have a great lead in no time.

A few of the people to ask and sources to turn to are:

Your parents. They may know someone (or know someone who knows someone) who has just the kind of job you're looking for.

Your friends and neighbors. You might be surprised to find out how many interesting jobs these people have when you start asking them what they (or their parents) do for a living.

Librarians. Since you've already figured out what kinds of companies employ people in your field of interest, the next step is to ask for information about local employers. Although it's a bit cumbersome to use, a big volume called *Contacts Influential* can provide this kind of information.

Professional associations. Call, e-mail, or write to the professional associations you discovered using the activity on pages 159 to 161 and ask for recommendations.

Chambers of commerce. The local chamber of commerce probably has a directory of employers, their specialties, and their phone numbers. Call the chamber, explain what you are looking for, and give them a chance to help their future workforce.

Newspaper and magazine articles. Find an article about the subject you are interested in. Chances are pretty good that it will mention the name of at least one expert in the field. The article probably won't include the person's phone number (that would be too easy), so you'll have to look for clues. Common clues include the name of the company that they work for, the town that they live in, and, if the person is an author, the name of their publisher. Make a few phone calls and track them down (if long distance calls are involved, make sure to get your parents' permission first).

INQUIRING KIDS WANT TO KNOW

Before you make the call, make a list of questions to ask. You'll cover more ground if you focus on using the five Ws (and the H) that you've probably heard about in your creative writing classes: Who? What? Where? When? How? and Why? For example:

1. Whom do you work for?

   ____

2. What is a typical workday like for you?

   ____

3. Where can I get some on-the-job experience?

   ____

4. When did you become a ________________________?
(profession)

5. How much can you earn in this profession? (But remember, it's not polite to ask someone how much *he* or *she* earns.)

____

6. Why did you choose this profession?

____

Use a grid like the one below to keep track of the questions you ask in the boxes labeled "Q" and the answers you receive in the boxes labeled "A."

Who?	What?	Where?	When?	How?	Why?
Q	Q	Q	Q	Q	Q
A	A	A	A	A	A
Q	Q	Q	Q	Q	Q
A	A	A	A	A	A

One last suggestion: Add a professional (and very classy) touch to the interview process by following up with a thank-you note to the person who took time out of a busy schedule to talk with you.

#6 INFORMATION IS POWER

As you may have noticed, a similar pattern of information was used for each of the careers profiled in this book. Each entry included:

- a general description of the career
- Try It Out activities to give readers a chance to find out what it's really like to do each job
- a list of Web sites, library resources, and professional organizations to check for more information
- a get-acquainted interview with a professional

You may have also noticed that all the information you just gathered would fit rather nicely in a Career Ideas for Kids career profile of your own. Just fill in the blanks on the following pages to get your thoughts together (or, if this book does not belong to you, use a separate sheet of paper).

And by the way, this formula is one that you can use throughout your life to help you make fully informed career choices.

CAREER TITLE ______________________

WHAT IS A ____________________ ?

Use career encyclopedias and other resources to write a description of this career.

____

____

____

____

SKILL SET

✔ ________

✔ ________

✔ ________

TRY IT OUT

Write project ideas here. Ask your parents and your teacher to come up with a plan.

____

____

____

____

____

CHECK IT OUT

ON THE WEB

List Internet addresses of interesting Web sites you find.

____

____

____

____

____

AT THE LIBRARY

List the titles and authors of books about this career.

WITH THE EXPERTS

List professional organizations where you can learn more about this profession.

GET ACQUAINTED

Interview a professional in the field and summarize your findings.

Whoa, everybody! At this point, you've put in some serious miles on your career exploration journey. Before you move on, let's put things in reverse for just a sec and take another look at some of the clues you uncovered about yourself when you completed the "Discover" activities in the Get in Gear chapter on pages 6 to 25.

The following activities will help lay the clues you learned about yourself alongside the clues you learned about a favorite career idea. The comparison will help you decide if that particular career idea is a good idea for you to pursue. It doesn't matter if a certain career sounds absolutely amazing. If it doesn't honor your skills, your interests, and your values, it's not going to work for you.

The first time you looked at these activities, they were numbered one through five as "Discover" activities. This time around they are numbered in the same order but labeled "Rediscover" activities. That's not done to confuse you (sure hope it doesn't!). Instead, it's done to drive home a very important point that this is an important process you'll want to revisit time and time again as you venture throughout your career—now and later.

First, pick the one career idea that you are most interested in at this point and write its name here (or if this book doesn't belong to you, blah, blah, blah—you know the drill by now):

____

With that idea in mind, revisit your responses to the following Get in Gear activities and complete the following:

REDISCOVER #1: WATCH FOR SIGNS ALONG THE WAY

Based on your responses to the statements on page 7, choose which of the following road signs best describes how you feel about your career idea:

- Green light—Go! Go! Go! This career idea is a perfect fit!
- Yellow light—Proceed with caution! This career idea is a good possibility, but you're not quite sure that it's the "one" just yet.
- Stop—Hit the brakes! There's no doubt about it—this career idea is definitely not for you!

REDISCOVER #2: RULES OF THE ROAD

Take another look at the work-values chart you made on page 15. Now use the same symbols to create a work-values chart for the career idea you are considering. After you have all the symbols in place, compare the two charts and answer these questions:

- Does your career idea's **purpose** line up with yours? Would it allow you to work in the kind of **place** you most want to work in?
- What about the **time** commitment—is it in sync with what you're hoping for?
- Does it let you work with the **tools** and the kind of **people** you most want to work with?
- And, last but not least, are you willing to do what it takes to **prepare** for a career like this?

PURPOSE	PLACE	TIME
TOOLS	**PEOPLE**	**PREPARATION**

REDISCOVER #3: DANGEROUS DETOURS

Go back to page 15 and double-check your list of 10 careers that you hope to avoid at any cost.

Is this career on that list? _____Yes _____ No

Should it be? _____Yes _____ No

REDISCOVER #4: ULTIMATE CAREER DESTINATION

Pull out the ultimate career destination brochure you made (as described on page 16). Use a pencil to cross through every reference to "my ideal career" and replace it with the name of the career idea you are now considering.

Is the brochure still true? ____Yes ____ No

If not, what would you change on the brochure to make it true?

REDISCOVER #5: GET SOME DIRECTION

Quick! Think fast! What is your personal Skill Set as discovered on page 25?

Write down your top three interest areas:

1. ______________________________

2. ______________________________

3. ______________________________

What three interest areas are most closely associated with your career idea?

1. ______________________________

2. ______________________________

3. ______________________________

Does this career's interest areas match any of yours?
____Yes ____ No

Now the big question: Are you headed in the right direction?

If so, here are some suggestions to keep you moving ahead:

- Keep learning all you can about this career—read, surf the Web, talk to people, and so on. In other words, keep using some of the strategies you used in the Don't Stop Now chapter on pages 153 to 167 to do all you can to make a fully informed career decision.
- Work hard in school and get good grades. What you do now counts! Your performance, your behavior, your attitude—all conspire to either propel you forward or hold you back.
- Get involved in clubs and other after-school activities to further develop your interests and skills. Whether it's student government, 4-H, or sports, these kinds of activities give you a chance to try new things and gain confidence in your abilities.

If not, here are some suggestions to help you regroup:

- Read other books in the Career Ideas for Kids series to explore options associated with your other interest areas.
- Take a variety of classes in school and get involved in different kinds of after-school activities to get a better sense of what you like and what you do well.
- Talk to your school guidance counselor about taking a career assessment test to help fine-tune your focus.
- Most of all, remember that time is on your side. Use the next few years to discover more about yourself, explore the options, and experiment with what it will take to make you succeed. Keep at it and look forward to a fantastic future!

This has been quite a trip. If someone tries to tell you that this process is easy, don't believe them. Figuring out what you want to do with the rest of your life is heavy stuff, and it should be. If you don't put some thought (and some sweat and hard work) into the process, you'll get stuck with whatever comes your way.

You may not have things planned to a T. Actually, it's probably better if you don't. You'll change some of your ideas as you grow and experience new things. And, you may find an interesting detour or two along the way. That's okay.

The most important thing about beginning this process now is that you've started to dream. You've discovered that you have some unique talents and abilities to share. You've become aware of some of the ways you can use them to make a living—and perhaps make a difference in the world.

Whatever you do, don't lose sight of the hopes and dreams you've discovered. You've got your entire future ahead of you. Use it wisely.

PASSPORT TO YOUR FUTURE

Getting where you want to go requires patience, focus, and lots of hard work. It also hinges on making good choices. Following is a list of some surefire ways to give yourself the best shot at a bright future. Are you up to the challenge? Can you do it? Do you dare?

Put your initials next to each item that you absolutely promise to do.

___ Do my best in every class at school

___ Take advantage of every opportunity to get a wide variety of experiences through participation in sports, after-school activities, at my favorite place of worship, and in my community

___ Ask my parents, teachers, or other trusted adults for help when I need it

___ Stay away from drugs, alcohol, and other bad scenes that can rob me of a future before I even get there

___ Graduate from high school

SOME FUTURE DESTINATIONS

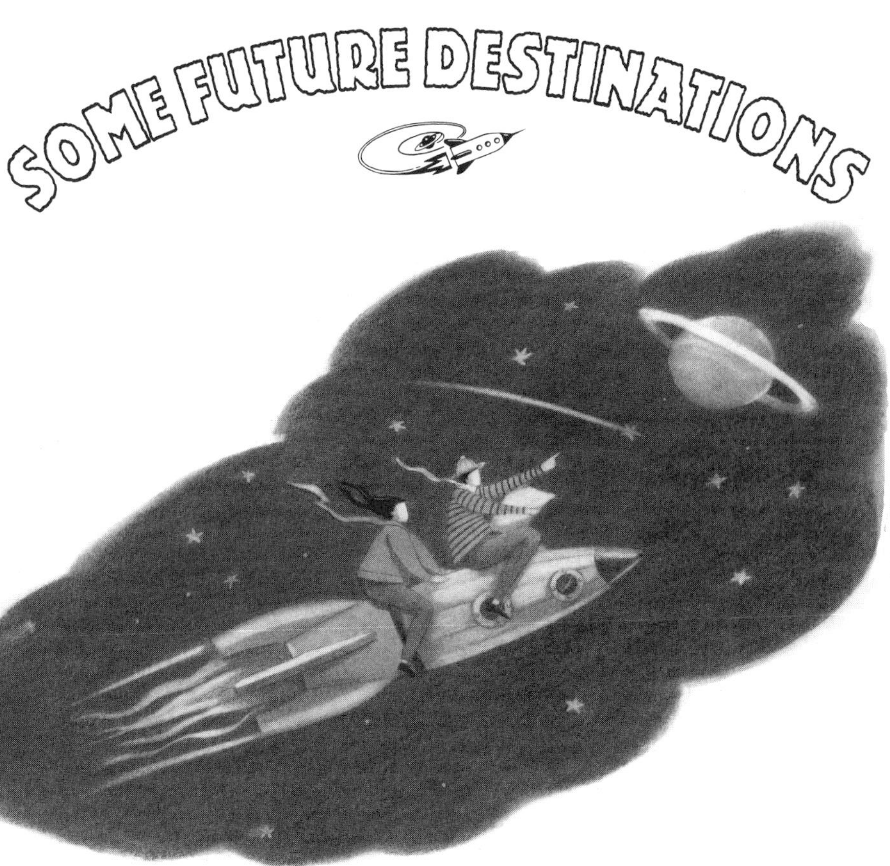

Wow! Look how far you've come! By now you should be well-equipped to discover, explore, and experiment your way to an absolutely fantastic future. To keep you headed in the right direction, this section will point you toward useful resources that provide more insight, information, and inspiration as you continue your quest to find the perfect career.

IT'S NOT JUST FOR NERDS

The school counselor's office is not just a place where teachers send troublemakers. One of its main purposes is to help students like you make the most of your educational opportunities. Most schools will have a number of useful resources, including career assessment tools (ask about the Self-Directed Search Career Explorer or the COPS Interest

Inventory—these are especially useful assessments for people your age). They may also have a stash of books, videos, and other helpful materials.

Make sure no one's looking and sneak into your school counseling office to get some expert advice!

AWESOME INTERNET CAREER RESOURCES

Your parents will be green with envy when they see all the career planning resources you have at your fingertips. Get ready to hear them whine, "But they didn't have all this stuff when I was a kid." Make the most of these cyberspace opportunities.

- **Adventures in Education**
  http://adventuresineducation.org/middleschool
  Here you'll find some useful tools to make the most of your education—starting now. Make sure to watch "The Great College Mystery," an online animation featuring Dr. Ed.

- **America's Career InfoNet**
  http://www.acinet.org
  Career sites don't get any bigger than this one! Compliments of the U.S. Department of Labor, and a chunk of your parent's tax dollars, you'll find all kinds of information about what people do, how much money they make, and where they work. Although it's mostly geared toward adults, you may want to take a look at some of the videos (the site has links to more than 450!) that show people at work.

- **ASVAB Career Exploration Program**
  http://www.asvabprogram.com
  This site may prove especially useful as you continue to think through various options. It includes sections

for students to learn about themselves, to explore careers, and to plan for their futures.

Career Voyages
http://www.careervoyages.gov
This site will be especially helpful to you as you get a little older. It offers four paths to get you started: "Where do I start?" "Which industries are growing?" "How do I qualify and get a job?" and "Does education pay? How do I pay?" However, it also includes a special section especially for elementary school students. Just click the button that says "Still in elementary school?" or go to http://www.careervoyages.gov/students-elementary.cfm.

Job Profiles
http://jobprofiles.org
This site presents the personal side of work with profiles of people working in jobs associated with agriculture and nature, arts and sports, business and communications, construction and manufacturing, education and science, government, health and social services, retail and wholesale, and other industries.

Major and Careers Central
http://www.collegeboard.com/csearch/majors_careers
This site is hosted by the College Board (the organization responsible for a very important test called the SAT, which you're likely to encounter if you plan to go to college). It includes helpful information about how different kinds of subjects you can study in college can prepare you for specific types of jobs.

Mapping Your Future
http://mapping-your-future.org/MHSS

This site provides strategies and resources for students as they progress through middle school and high school.

- **My Cool Career**
  http://www.mycoolcareer.com
  This site is where you can take free online self-assessment quizzes, explore your dreams, and listen to people with interesting jobs talk about their work.

- **O*NET Online**
  http://online.onetcenter.org
  This U.S. Department of Labor site provides comprehensive information about hundreds of important occupations. Although you may need to ask a parent or teacher to help you figure out how to use the system, it can be a good source of digging for nitty-gritty details about a specific type of job. For instance, each profile includes a description of the skills, abilities, and special knowledge needed to perform each job.

- **Think College Early**
  http://www.ed.gov/students/prep/college/thinkcollege/early/edlite-tcehome.html
  Even though you almost need a college degree just to type the Web address for this U.S. Department of Education site, it contains some really cool career information and helps you think about how college might fit into your future plans.

- **What Interests you?**
  http://www.bls.gov/k12
  This Bureau of Labor Statistics site is geared toward students. It lets you explore careers by interests such as reading, building and fixing things, managing money, helping people, and more.

JOIN THE CLUB

Once you've completed eighth grade, you are eligible to check out local opportunities to participate in Learning for Life's career education programs. Some communities offer Explorer posts that sponsor activities with students interested in industries that include the arts and humanities, aviation, business, communications, engineering, fire service, health, law enforcement, law and government, science, skilled trades, or social services. To find a local office, go to http://www.learning-for-life.org/exploring/main.html and type your zip code.

Until then, you can go online and play *Life Choices*, a really fun and challenging game where you get one of five virtual jobs at http://www.learning-for-life.org/games/LCSH/index.html.

MORE CAREER BOOKS ESPECIALLY FOR KIDS

It's especially important that people your age find out all they can about as many different careers as they can. Books like the ones listed below can introduce all kinds of interesting ideas that you might not encounter in your everyday life.

Greenfeld, Barbara C., and Robert A. Weinstein. *The Kids' College Almanac: A First Look at College*. 3d ed. Indianapolis, Ind.: JIST Works, 2005.

Young Person's Occupational Outlook Handbook. 5th ed. Indianapolis, Ind.: JIST Works, 2004.

Following are brief descriptions of several series of books geared especially toward kids like you. To find copies of these books, ask your school or public librarian to help you search the library computer system using the name of the series.

Career Connections (published by UXL)
This extensive series features information and illustrations about jobs of interest to people interested in art and design, entrepreneurship, food, government and law, history, math and computers, and the performing arts as well as those who want to work with their hands or with living things.

Career Ideas for Kids (written by Diane Lindsey Reeves, published by Ferguson)
This series of interactive career exploration books features 10 different titles for kids who like adventure and travel, animals and nature, art, computers, math and money, music and dance, science, sports, talking, and writing.

Careers Without College (published by Peterson's)
These books offer a look at options available to those who prefer to find jobs that do not require a college degree and include titles focusing on cars, computers, fashion, fitness, health care, and music.

Cool Careers (published by Rosen Publishing)
Each title in this series focuses on a cutting-edge occupation such as computer animator, hardware engineer, multimedia and new media developer, video game designer, Web entrepreneur, and webmaster.

Discovering Careers for Your Future (published by Ferguson)
This series includes a wide range of titles that include those that focus on adventure, art, construction, fashion, film, history, nature, publishing, and radio and television.

Risky Business (written by Keith Elliot Greenberg, published by Blackbirch Press)
These books feature stories about people with adventurous types of jobs and include titles about a bomb squad officer, disease detective, marine biologist, photojournalist, rodeo clown, smoke jumper, storm chaser, stunt woman, test pilot, and wildlife special agent.

HEAVY-DUTY RESOURCES

Career encyclopedias provide general information about a lot of professions and can be a great place to start a career search. Those listed here are easy to use and provide useful information about nearly a zillion different jobs. Look for them in the reference section of your local library.

Career Discovery Encyclopedia, 6th ed. New York: Ferguson, 2006.

Careers for the 21st Century. Farmington Hills, Mich.: Lucent Books, 2002.

Children's Dictionary of Occupations. Princeton, N.J.: Cambridge Educational, 2004.

Encyclopedia of Career and Vocational Guidance. New York: Ferguson, 2005.

Farr, Michael, and Laurence Shatkin. *Enhanced Occupational Outlook Handbook.* Indianapolis, Ind.: JIST Works, 2006.

Occupational Outlook Handbook. Washington, D.C.: U.S. Government Printing Office, 2006.

FINDING PLACES TO WORK

Even though you probably aren't quite yet in the market for a real job, you can learn a lot about the kinds of jobs you might find if you were looking by visiting some of the most popular job-hunting sites on the Internet. Two particularly good ones to investigate are America's Job Bank (http://www.ajb.org) and Monster (http://www.monster.com).

INDEX

Page numbers in **boldface** indicate main articles. Page numbers in *italics* indicate photographs.